Why Fly

BY THE SAME AUTHOR

Tough Broad: From Bird-Watching to BASE Jumping—How Outdoor Adventure Improves Our Lives as We Age

A Little Tea Book: All the Essentials from Leaf to Cup
(with Sebastian Beckwith)

You Are Mighty: A Guide to Changing the World

The Gutsy Girl: Escapades for Your Life of Epic Adventure

Lost Cat: A True Story of Love, Desperation, and GPS Technology

Fighting Fire

East Wind, Rain

Why Fly

SEEKING AWE, HEALING,
AND OUR TRUE SELVES
IN THE SKY

CAROLINE PAUL

BLOOMSBURY PUBLISHING
NEW YORK · LONDON · OXFORD · NEW DELHI · SYDNEY

BLOOMSBURY PUBLISHING
Bloomsbury Publishing Inc.
1359 Broadway, New York, NY 10018, USA
50 Bedford Square, London, WC1B 3DP, UK
Bloomsbury Publishing Ireland Limited,
29 Earlsfort Terrace, Dublin 2, D02 AY28, Ireland

BLOOMSBURY, BLOOMSBURY PUBLISHING, and the Diana logo
are trademarks of Bloomsbury Publishing Plc

First published in the United States 2026

Copyright © Caroline Paul, 2026

All rights reserved. No part of this publication may be: i) reproduced or transmitted in any form, electronic or mechanical, including photocopying, recording or by means of any information storage or retrieval system without prior permission in writing from the publishers; or ii) used or reproduced in any way for the training, development or operation of artificial intelligence (AI) technologies, including generative AI technologies. The rights holders expressly reserve this publication from the text and data mining exception as per Article 4(3) of the Digital Single Market Directive (EU) 2019/790

Bloomsbury Publishing Plc does not have any control over, or responsibility for, any third-party websites referred to or in this book. All internet addresses given in this book were correct at the time of going to press. The author and publisher regret any inconvenience caused if addresses have changed or sites have ceased to exist, but can accept no responsibility for any such changes.

ISBN: HB: 978-1-63973-499-3; EBOOK: 978-1-63973-500-6

Library of Congress Cataloging-in-Publication Data is available

2 4 6 8 10 9 7 5 3 1

Typesetting by Six Red Marbles India
Printed in the United States by Lakeside Book Company

To find out more about our authors and books visit www.bloomsbury.com
and sign up for our newsletters.

Bloomsbury books may be purchased for business or promotional use. For information on bulk purchases please contact Macmillan Corporate and Premium Sales Department at specialmarkets@macmillan.com.

For product safety-related questions contact productsafety@bloomsbury.com

To Wendy

CONTENTS

PART 1. EARTH OR SKY

  1. Sky   3

PART 2. PREFLIGHT

  2. Gravity   11
  3. Checklists   15

PART 3. TAXI

  4. How Flight Works (Because It Does)   27
  5. Drag   35
  6. A Short, Incomplete History of Flight   39
  7. Airborne   47

PART 4. TAKEOFF

  8. Lift   57
  9. Gliders   61
  10. Migration   69
  11. The Pioneers   77
  12. Loneliness   83
  13. Fear of Flying   89

PART 5. FLIGHT (OUTBOUND)

14. The View	97
15. Low and Slow	103
16. Birds	113
17. Maps	123
18. The Controls	135
19. Navigation	141

PART 6. FLIGHT (INBOUND)

20. Weather	153
21. Groundspeed	167
22. Airspeed	173
23. Pilot Error	181

PART 7. LANDING

24. Traffic Pattern	191
25. Communication	201
26. Landing: You Can Do It Too	209
27. Final Approach	217
28. Touchdown	219
29. Hangar	229
Acknowledgments	231
Notes	233

PART 1

EARTH OR SKY

> *I want*
> *to think again of dangerous and noble things.*
> *I want to be light and frolicsome.*
> *I want to be improbable, beautiful, and afraid of nothing,*
> *as though I had wings.*
>
> — MARY OLIVER, "STARLINGS IN WINTER"

I

Sky

I'm flying low over scrubby California hills of trees and granite when my engine cuts out. This is a rinky-dink aircraft, just a single seat on wheels suspended under a hang glider wing, powered by the kind of motor also used for, say, weed whackers. The motor turns a propeller, but now, sadly, the propeller no longer spins. All that's left for me is a dubious glide ratio and something close to a miracle.

I have practiced the dreaded engine-out scenario many times; still, when it actually happens my stomach drops in that *Oh-no* way for which one can never really be prepared. My mind blanks out at the sudden silence. Then there's a moment of pure adrenaline— the beating heart, the closed throat, the frazzled synapses. Finally reasoning begins to defibrillate its quivering, disassembled pieces— *Is this? Why is? For when?*—into a more coherent whole. My options, which are limited, pop off like fireworks in my brain.

Try. Start. Engine.

Or (now my brain is clearing): *Forget the engine. Look for a place to land.*

It's tempting to go through the steps to restart, but I'm only a thousand feet up, and this is how pilots die, using up the little time they have on a fool's errand. There is no guarantee that my already finicky two-stroke will come to life, and if it doesn't it will be too late to find an open field. I swing my head wildly, knowing I'd clocked a landing zone before the engine quit, because that's what you do as a pilot of experimental planes like the one I'm flying—always look for somewhere to put down, just in case. Now *just in case* is here, and the spot is not as friendly as it looked when I didn't think I actually needed it; it's an incline hemmed in by trees, making for a nearly impossible feat.

Dear Reader, I'm not dropping like a stone. A hang glider wing wants to fly. But it has the weight of its pilot and the frame on which she sits as well as that traitorous engine underneath, so I'm losing altitude quickly. I must make a decision and so I do: a field within reach between two hills, seemingly clean of rocks and flat enough. I remind myself I have the height to set up as for any other runway—it'll be a short downwind leg, then base leg, then final approach. I make my first shallow turn. I crane my neck so I can keep my eyes on my touchdown point (*Look where you want to go* is a maxim that works in the air as in life). But are those rocks? Is that a gnarly bush? Are there crosswinds? It's too late to change my mind so I tell myself to focus, even as another part of me smirks *You are so in trouble now.*

I've flown Cessnas and paragliders, so I'm not new to unplanned events in the air, or things going wrong, or even things going terribly wrong. But if I'm making this sound like a linear progression of thought and sound judgment, it is not. My brain discusses the current situation in the foreground, but behind there is a strange

Sky

playlist of observations and thoughts: I'm aware that my nose is running, say; that the sky is very blue. I flash on the faces of my family, and my cat. But my rational brain is now flexing and snarling, playing a mean bouncer. These useless thoughts waft in and out like dim shadows against a velvet rope, denied entry.

Did I mention that I have less than ten hours of flying time in this ultralight "trike" (technically called a "weight shift control trike," with the word trike referring to the three wheels underneath me) since my certification was granted? And that the term "certification" is an overstatement for an aircraft (also an overstatement) that isn't formally recognized by the boss of civil aviation, the Federal Aviation Administration? In a few years the FAA will perk up and crack down and everyone will have to study regulations and pass tests, but right now trikes like the one I fly are filed under NUISANCE and WILD WEST and REALLY??? and pushed into a dusty cabinet somewhere and left alone.

I bank left for the base leg and then left again for the final approach. The wind is calm. The field, however, is not perfect. I can see now that it has hillocks and mounds and deep scours. (Later I will realize that it's pocked with hoofprints, the winter mud curdled by cows during the rains and now hardened into cement-like soil under the summer sun.)

My heart molts an outer layer, getting smaller in my chest.

To land without an engine is the truest of commitments and I must do the best I can with the choice I've made. I grit my teeth. I exhale sharply. I keep my elbows at my sides as I hold/grip/strangle the control bar because someone once said that doing this keeps the arms as relaxed as possible. But still my shoulders rise to my ears.

On the final leg the imperfect field looms up before me. I can feel a part of me unraveling, wanting to close my eyes and just land (this urge is known among pilots as *get-on-the-ground-itis*), but another part of me is steely. The steely part wins out and I instead pin my eyes to the touchdown point. My tasks have been narrowed to only a few simple but precarious objectives: Don't overshoot into trees. Don't undershoot into the fence. Come in fast enough to counter any errant wind (speed is key to avoiding the dreaded stall) and yet slow enough to touch down lightly. My jaw is clamped tight. I'm sweating for real. I remind myself I've practiced this a ton of times. *Easy peasy. Pleasy, pleasy.*

The wheels hover, about to meet the earth. It's beyond my planned touchdown but fine, just fine, as long as we land soon. Then the ground is here. The trike and I bounce side to side violently, at the mercy of ghost cows, cows who no doubt loved this field and stamped and tramped with great delight months ago. I think *Please don't pop a tire, snap an axle, shear a bolt*, but really who am I to ask for more than a safe landing?

I come to a quick stop. It's so quiet, except for my breathing. The trike is intact. I get out stiffly, take off my helmet, look around. I do the thing that people do when they come out the other side of danger—I laugh loudly, shake my head, then kneel on the ground and touch it. I'm feeling dramatic, I guess. And why not? There's no one around to see. I stand up and wonder how the hell I'm going to get out of here. I have a rudimentary aviation radio that might or might not get reception; it's the era of flip phones and spotty coverage. Perhaps I will walk. Perhaps the ultralight will restart. But for now, everything important has been resolved. The grass is shining, the undulating ground is a pattern of beauty. I'm safe, I'm alive. That's enough.

Afterward, there are the inevitable questions. Mostly they cover the logistics of the incident (how did this situation occur; how could this have been avoided?). But they also go deeper.

Is flying worth it? a pilot asks herself (her family and friends ask that too, over and over, sometimes with hysteria in their voices). Yes, worth it. I chalk the experience up to a valuable lesson in so many things—decision-making skills, maintenance, off-field landings. I also eventually upgrade my experimental flying machine after it's clear that this one has been assembled by an amateur kit builder who likes to put items in upside down. (It also has a two-stroke engine with a disclaimer in the owner's manual that begins "This engine, by its design, is subject to sudden stoppage . . . It has not received any safety or durability testing and conforms to no aircraft standards.")

The pilot Tom Black, who made his name in the 1930s with seat-of-the-pants flying in East Africa and a series of dashing long-distance flights, once remarked that flight makes "you feel that everything you see belongs to you—all the pieces are put together and the whole is yours . . . It makes you feel bigger than you are and closer to being something you've sensed you might be capable of, but never had the courage to seriously imagine."

For me, it's the opposite. Flight makes me feel as if I own nothing at all. The sky is wide and indifferent, amniotic, and I float there, tethered, tiny, stunned. I am puny and insignificant, but somehow not unimportant. There are bigger forces at work, mercurial and mysterious.

This may be what the mail pilot Antoine de Saint-Exupéry (and famous author of *The Little Prince*) thought about flying too, though it's difficult to puzzle through his overwrought style, which works hair-raisingly well when he narrates an encounter, say, with a cyclone that almost tore the wings off his plane (which he details in his memoir *Wind, Sand, and Stars*), but when he writes of why pilots fly, things get murky. "And then, only, from the height of our rectilinear trajectories, do we discover the essential foundation, that fundament of rock and sand and salt in which here and there and from time to time life like a little moss in crevices of ruins has risked its precarious existence," he intones. Maybe that's true, M. de Saint-Exupéry, but I must be honest, reading that passage felt like being pummeled by a word cyclone that almost tore my brain from my head.

Then again, sometimes the pure beauty and mystery of flight defy language itself.

You may be a certified pilot; chances are you are not (2024 FAA records show that certified pilots make up a mere 0.15 percent of the total U.S. population). Most likely, though, you are one of the five billion people around the world who board a passenger plane every year. You see flight as romantic, or terrifying, or a modern convenience to be tolerated. Whatever attitude you hold, you have asked yourself at some point, *Why*. Why fly? We are landlubbers. We are two-legged featherless creatures. Gravity, not lift, is our natural fate.

Or is it?

We have been reaching for flight for centuries—from unwieldy balloons to rickety gliders to prop planes to jets. We willingly load ourselves into long metal tubes, waving tickets to places like Des Moines, Medford, Glendive, Deadhorse. We dream of jet packs, then discard them. We hope for flying cars. We divert, seeking simpler designs, to paragliders and paramotors and gyrocopters and wing suits and even back to balloons, setting solo around-the-world records and even jumping off the lip of one from the stratosphere, 110,000 feet up. Along the way we flub, we crash-land, we simply crash. Still, we want to fly.

But *why?* you ask again. *Why fly?*

PART 2

PREFLIGHT

I fly because it releases my mind from the tyranny of petty things.

A<small>NTOINE DE</small> S<small>AINT</small>-E<small>XUPÉRY</small>

2

Gravity

The year that my marriage begins to fray in earnest, I become obsessed with flight. I am not a new pilot; I have been flying various aircraft all my life. I've always liked to be aloft but I am not consumed with it, not yet. Then, at fifty-eight years old, I find myself racking up the flying hours in ways I never had with the Cessna I learned when I was just twenty, the paraglider I picked up in my thirties, and that dastardly motorized hang glider that I piloted from my forties onward. This ardor is new.

I begin to fly a gyrocopter.

The reasons for this aren't all mysterious. It's easier to learn a landing than a human heart. It's easier to check the oil and look for the fill line. You add oil, or not. When the weather is bad, you don't have to stick it out. You close the hangar door and leave. You'll fly another day.

But still, it's a strange decision. My heart has a hole that needs filling and I decide to fill it with a strange-looking piece of metal that resembles a tiny helicopter. The hard edges and wires and rotors shouldn't have fitted, for one. Pilots are often intrigued with the mechanical; they love the bright aluminum and wires and baffles and spark plugs, the additions that promise high speeds and bigger numbers. Not me. I have no engineering mind, have little in common with those who tinker with their plane to make it snazzier. I don't tinker at all. Sometimes I rue the fact that I have to be held up by a structure of any sort and wish I could just fly like the birds. But my marriage is in trouble and I don't know how to fix it but I can get better at flying so that is what I do. And I pick a gyrocopter to do it in.

Flying and love have something in common. For one, they both feel like magic. Yet both are governed by simple science—physics and oxytocin respectively. Still, no one new to either really believes that when you tell them. Even today when I review the Bernoulli effect and Newton's Third Law of Motion—the natural laws responsible for getting the heaviest of airliners into the sky—it seems that a key ingredient is missing in the explanation, and it includes the word *miracle*.

I arrive at my hangar and push the doors open. In sections, the day tumbles in. My little yellow flying machine goes from jagged shadow to awash with light, and as it does, the gray in my mind shifts just a little. How can I not feel gladness for this result of someone's fantastical, perhaps slightly tipsy, dream: a large rotor attached like a wide-brimmed hat to what looks like a go-kart. I have traded a hang glider wing for one long helicopter-like blade. Otherwise, everything else is similar to the ultralight aircraft that dropped me into that cow field almost two decades ago. But it is improved upon: Instead of a five-gallon tank, my gyrocopter carries almost twenty. It has a seat for a passenger, and another two pistons that make it a worthy four-stroke engine, a significant improvement on the twitchy two-stroke I had before. There is a fancy radio that reaches over mountains, a switch for fuel and another for lights. On the panel are gauges that read airspeed and exhaust temperatures, oil temperature and altitude.

Come to think of it, that first trike had no panel instruments at all except an airspeed indicator, which was not located on the panel but attached manually to the hang glider bar so it could be seen. It was impossibly rudimentary, just a chintzy plastic tube in which an air bubble bounced along a grid of numbers in response to the incoming wind. This sparse instrumentation reminds that for most aircraft, airspeed really is the only important number to know, and that only eight or so decades ago there were often no instruments at all, and airspeed was judged by the vibration of the stick along with the sound of the wind. Low vibration, lots of wind noise: good. High vibration, much too quiet: the dreaded stall was imminent. Still, as flying technologies advance, so do our panels. These luxuries add weight, both metaphorical and literal; the bells and whistles make the craft seem more trustworthy, as well as no longer "ultralight." But it's still everything I love about flying: an open cockpit, an avian feel. Don't be fooled by its clumsy name—gyrocopter/gyroplane (often shortened to the less clumsy *gyro*)—and the ungainly resemblance to a praying mantis. It's a thing of beauty and promise to me.

The promise is so many things—adventure, a different perspective, poetics. But today the promise is *escape*. Be a different creature entirely—why not? That creature: winged, with wheels for feet, and a voice that cries, not in whimpers or the strange gulps of the newly bereaved, but in howling, baying, confident roars. *Up, up, and away*, I think now with hands on hips and head cocked. That classic song, that hearty chant. The *up* beckons: Sky, heaven, fullness, that loveliness of possibility. But it is not the up that resonates with me now, it is the *away*, a word that sounds like the wind and that snatches the very last sound of itself, as if you are already gone before the syllable has ended.

3

Checklists

Alarm horns, airspeed maxes and minimums, gauge alerts, and sudden bank angles—all these warn of an emergency in the air. But what instruments are present for marriage? Both of us had thought we'd done our homework, inspected for sturdiness and longevity. We knew that the journey would not be turbulent-free but certainly, we assured each other, it would be safe from great mishap and harm.

For an aircraft there's a simple procedure to avert disaster: the preflight inspection. We call it colloquially "the walk-around," or just *preflight*, that close look at every part and piece to make sure each is in good condition, that nothing is in need of care, that everything is in order, that things will go as implicitly promised. There is no such equivalent for relationships—or perhaps there is, a slow do-si-do with the beloved, arm outstretched, fingers touching, and a simple statement of *I am listening*. But this is ongoing maintenance we had both clearly begun to ignore.

Ironically, while I may have gotten careless with the main human in my life, this is a procedure I never shirk with my aircraft. From the workhorse Cessna 150 to this gangly insect of a machine, preflight is a nonnegotiable first step before each flight. And so I start: the lingering, gazing, patting, prodding, twisting of caps and pushing of buttons, tugging of wires, fist-bumping of exhaust pipes, and gentle pull on every surface to make sure it won't part from the aircraft and hit the propeller.

In my hand is a checklist. This pilot checklist is mandatory, no matter how long you've been flying or how expert you are, though this astonishes many people. Take the friend who regaled me recently about a prop plane trip she had taken. The pilot had looked so young, she told me. She doubted he had graduated from college. "And then he needed a piece of paper to start the engine!" she exclaimed, horrified, and didn't listen when I assured her that this meant she had been in very good hands. Many pilots, especially those in my flying world—of strange "experimental" craft—ignore the rules and eschew the checklist just as they did the regulations, certifications, and training that once weren't a requirement for what we flew. But they do so at their own peril.

The checklist was invented in 1919 by the U.S. Postal Service, now considered an antiquated bureaucracy but then surprisingly ahead of their time. They embraced the airplane when other government arms (like the military!) were dismissing the technology. They quickly realized that its increasing complexity required some sort of reminder for their (stressed, tired) pilots; this was an era when there were *fourteen steps* needed to simply fire up the engine of the DH-4 Liberty postal plane. And these fourteen steps came after the thorough inspection of fuselage, wings, wing wires, propeller, electrical wires, controls, hydraulic tubes, instruments, tires, and individual engine parts. The checklist was born.

These days I physically clutch the laminated paper and make my eyes move across the words, even after so many years. I have no illusions about my own brain and its willingness to gloss quickly over some details and drop others completely in its daily fight to get me through the day. The checklist, like a conscientious school crossing guard, knows that we are overconfident animals, true believers in our own good fortune and the corrective power of expertise and experience. It understands that we are pummeled by choices and anesthetized by routine, that we are impatient multitaskers, mammals who fling ourselves headlong and heedless into our day. It knows we are wired to look for shortcuts, our neural system translating loose patterns into coherent wholes with lightning speed, which might be great for, say, outrunning a bear but truly sucks for flight, and probably for love as well. So here I am with a paper in hand, eyes darting to bullet point instructions on how to proceed and proceeding accordingly. Frankly it feels good. Finally a clear path. A proven route.

The physician and author Atul Gawande shares my enthusiasm, writing in the *New Yorker* about doctors at a certain hospital who, when performing a routine insertion of an intravenous line by memory alone, skipped at least one of the necessary steps in one third of their patients. These mistakes had ramifications: discomfort, infection, even death. At first a mishap like this seems understandable—medicine, after all, is so complicated. Consider, though, that this was a common procedure, and that there were *only five steps in total*. Once a checklist was used, Gawande notes, things quickly changed and infections dropped dramatically, from 11 percent to zero.

Why Fly

I love my checklist, though you can't tell by its oil stains, its crimped lamination, and, if it's the one I used for my trike, the two pages cinched together with a zip tie. With a checklist's help, I've found loose screws, detached air filter lines, and propeller dings. Once I found a nest of swallow eggs tucked into the hollow space of my hang glider wing (*wing: batons secure, struts secure, fabric—tears/wear/damage*). Overcome by fear that the mother bird wouldn't find the nest if I moved it, I instead transported the fragile cargo to a wild care center. When the eggs hatched, the sanctuary telephoned and asked where the nest had been found so the birds could be returned there. "In my wing," I told them, baffled. No, no, not the exact spot, they corrected, the location, the neighborhood. Birds, they explained, need to live in the environment their parents came from, because they learn a good deal of their birdsong while still in the egg. Different areas have different bird dialects; I gathered that relocating a young avian brood to the wrong place would be akin to plucking a six-year-old American from her Midwest hometown and asking her to navigate Italy.

There are other things that can be found in the nooks and crannies. After one takeoff, a cat emerged from the hollow wing area of a rudimentary fixed wing aircraft and stared down at the pilot and his passenger sitting in the open cockpit. The cat's fur whipped around in the wind, her expression a mix of dismay and annoyance, and she clung there, saved from sliding into oblivion only by a metal strut. The video was posted on the internet; in it one can see the pilot finally spotting the cat and initiating a gentle turn back to the airport so as not to dislodge his stowaway (all ends well). I imagine that after that, this pilot's preflight was more thorough.

A certain John Goddard, born in 1924, lived a life of adventures that ranged from exploring the Nile to landing a plane on an aircraft carrier to learning the violin. How could he lead such a colorful existence? He attributed it to a single moment when he was fifteen years old. He'd overheard an adult saying that he wished he were a boy again because he had not done what he thought he would with his life. Like a lightning strike Goddard suddenly understood how easy it was to get waylaid from one's dreams and decided then and there to write down everything he wanted to accomplish. The list grew over the years; by the time he died (of natural causes) he had completed 111 of its 127 items, among them retracing Marco Polo's expeditions, rafting the Congo, free diving to 40 feet while holding his breath for two and a half minutes, and typing 50 words a minute. Essentially, he was writing a preflight checklist for his life. I read this article in *National Geographic*, which arrived full of bright yellow promise at our house each month. I immediately began my own list. On it, along with being a whitewater rafting guide and writing a movie script (check, and check, though the script was terrible), was to become a pilot. I was twelve years old.

. . .

We have digressed. Do you remember where we are in the preflight? Probably not. The checklist tells me it's the oil cap— the fill line has been checked and the cap must now be returned to its place, or disaster will ensue. Glance at the page, make a mental check, and move to the next item.

A friend of mine once encountered a huge red-tailed hawk in her backyard. She and her son approached, and to their surprise he failed to fly away, just sat there peering at them with hooded eyes. Unsure whether the bird was rabid (later research informed them that birds can't get rabies, only mammals can) or simply cantankerous, they backed off and observed from a distance. He began to walk slowly toward them. Recognizing that this was unusual, the two humans scampered up their steep stairway into the house. The bird continued to follow, taking each step slowly and steadily, like some demon in a Stephen King novel. Was he hurt? Was he delivering a special message from the animal kingdom? Was he a reincarnated relative? At the top of the stairs the bird was halted by the glass door, so he simply waited there, staring at the *Homo sapiens* who cowered inside and even the dog that approached and stared back, baffled. (I've seen the photos. The situation is both hilarious and spooky.) Animal Care and Control officers finally showed up and explained that the hawk had probably eaten a large pigeon on the roof of the house. He'd then tried to fly off but, weighed down by the meal, he'd fallen to the ground instead, temporarily ringing his bird noggin. This didn't fully explain the weirdness of the hawk's behavior, but it made clear to me the importance of his future preflight checklist, which would remain short and simple: *Lunch—digested?*

It is worth noting that I fly "experimentals." This is a category of aircraft with multiple meanings to the FAA. Some may be in their nascent stages of design; others are simply aircraft pieced and parceled and welded and screwed by an amateur. All the trikes I flew were experimentals of the latter stripe, as is my gyrocopter. Technically this means that "the majority of parts have been fabricated and assembled by person(s) who undertakes the construction project solely for their own education or recreation." This is informally called the 51 percent rule, because the original owner must have performed at least 51 percent of the work, a definition that surely conjures images of a flying creature slapped together with screws from old cars, random bits of metal pulled from dumps, and canvas from tattered boat sails, as is the wont of mad tinkerers and inventors. But experimentals are decidedly not unsafe. These days the other 49 percent consists of labor and parts likely to come from respected factories that manufacture legitimate aircraft accessories and subject them to rigorous oversight. Experimentals also undergo yearly inspections, and their pilots are now mandated to hold certifications that promise skill and good judgment. Ultimately, much has changed since I first started flying experimental aircraft: once unregulated and barred from airports for fear of a crash on takeoff or parts dropped from its flimsy exoskeleton while in the traffic pattern, now they are commonplace and found in all classes of flying machine, from rotorcraft to glider to fixed wing to lighter-than-air.

. . .

Today I pick a flight ensemble that will ward off the cool April air, bundling up in not one, not two, but three coats, then pulling on my winter flight suit (open cockpit + 75 miles an hour + 1,000 feet or more = cold). I unzip its legs, rummage for the knee socks that I would never wear anywhere else and pull them over my jeans to seal my ankles, then zip the legs up again. Last, I add a neck warmer, then don the helmet so that by the time I am done dressing, my silhouette resembles more a snowdrift than an intrepid pilot.

After my first forced trike landing so many years ago, I'd packed a bag and secured it to the frame: chocks for the wheels, rope to tie the aircraft down in whatever field I might find myself in, extra carabiners because why not, duct tape because always, water for the long trek out, a paper map of the county to orient myself to the nearest road, and a fifty-dollar bill for the taxi I would have to flag down. These days all that seems antiquated.

Why Fly

Everything I need fits mostly into pockets, of which a flight suit has many: the lucky talismans (a quartz wing given by one friend for luck in the air, and a silver dollar with my birth year on it given by another), sunscreen, and of course duct tape, rolled unto itself, because all hail duct tape's wide range of powers. Then I drop my fully charged phone and a serrated folding knife into a pocket within reach and consider myself ready.

Most mornings the air is tattered with coastal fog. I peer out of the hangar repeatedly, gauging how much of the ceiling has lifted. I may even stroll toward the runway to check the windsock; I could call the automated weather station on my phone, but walking gives me an excuse to see if any other human is about, and what may be flying. Often it's just birds: Canada geese honking their outrage as they pass overhead, the dart of swallows among the hangar eaves. Sometimes there's a hawk making widening circles nearby. If there is a human, it's often someone in a pickup truck, white-haired, usually retired, Caucasian, male, who slows to ask whether I'm coming or going. I'll say *Going* and make a motion with my chin upward, and he'll make a similar jerk with his head to imply he is also clocking the weather. Then he'll say *It'll clear* if the fog is in, or *Looks good* if it's not, and I'll say *Yes*, and he'll say *Enjoy* and wave and drive off. I like these conversations, not for the words (obviously) but for the underlying meaning, which goes more like this: *Hi, pilot! I'm a pilot too, and I get how cool it is to be in the sky.* Sometimes the conversation will segue into a story, as on the morning Bob told me how he had been flying from San Francisco to Hawaii in his single engine something-or-other a few years back and the engine cut out and he had to ditch into the hearty Pacific Ocean, but not before he managed to yell his coordinates into his radio on the emergency channel, probably preceding them with

Mayday! Mayday! Mayday! (derived from the French *M'aidez*, which translates to "Help me.") He clung to a wing; when that sank, he dog-paddled a little while until a boat arrived. There may have been sharks, there may have been the exasperated sighs of a long-suffering wife, I can't remember. I do remember laughing and gasping throughout, because that is the way flying stories are told, that rat-tat-tat interchange of humor and terror that casts the pilot himself as a dumbass, though a lucky one.

Today no one is around at this early hour, and anyway I am eager to take to the runway in the peachy light. I put my checklist down, pat the pockets of my flight suit, grab my helmet, roll out my gyrocopter, and head to the burnished, waiting sky.

PART 3

TAXI

The bird is a machine . . . man has the capacity to create this machine. Such a machine lacks nothing but the bird's soul, which must be counterfeited by man.

LEONARDO DA VINCI

4

How Flight Works (Because It Does)

I am taxiing to Runway 29 today. The "taxi" is the pilot's final landbound movement, the aircraft in which she sits still more automobile than winged machine. The taxiway is even delineated by a yellow centerline, much as a road might be. Woe to you if your centerline is white; this means you are accidentally on the runway itself. Sometimes, though, an airport is so small that the runway does double as the taxiway, and you are always peering anxiously at the skies to make sure no incoming traffic is about to land on you.

    The hangars I now trundle past house all sorts of aircraft—refurbished warplanes, Beechcrafts, Piper Cubs, Cessnas, gyrocopters. There is even one large jet, which lumbers like a bear from its hulking den a few times a week, often loping to the nearest runway with little regard to prevailing traffic. Today, though, it's quiet. I key my mic anyway and ask for a radio check, a message that goes out to anyone in the vicinity with their own pilot radio on. This routine inquiry—part of the checklist, by the way—feels almost plaintive, a call less to check whether the message is scratchy or intermittent, and more simply a request for contact. *Hello? Anyone out there? Answer me, please.* Now there is just silence, which could mean a bad radio, or just that it's too early for most to be flying. Around me, only the birds are awake. They are darting and feinting. The circling hawk has landed and now sits on the taxiway sign, hunched as if in thought. Every so often the finial that is her head jerks side to side. But mostly she ignores me; she knows that I will be gone soon enough. I roll slowly past, then swing into the wind for the final run-up, all the while keeping an eye on my feathered colleague: Will she stay? Will she fly off? Birds in the vicinity of runways are always nerve-racking—a bird strike on takeoff could be catastrophic. But birds lazing on signs are also reminders: I am about to be in their territory. Be humble. Be careful. Go fly.

The number 29 is painted on the runway, I can see it out of the corner of my eye. It tells the pilot that when she begins her takeoff roll, she faces 290 degrees on the compass rose (west-northwest); if she starts on the other end of this single runway, she has a heading of 110 degrees (so that runway end is marked 11). Runways are built to face the area's prevailing winds, and ours come almost exclusively from the west, except when a storm is coming and then the wind swings southeasterly. Oddly, the airports on either side of mine and lying along the same valley tend to southeasterly winds even when ours blows two-niner.

I love this about wind, the way it seems to have a mind of its own. But this isn't caprice. Wind seems willy-nilly but it is not; it acts in earnest relationship to temperature changes and obstructions. That is why it's a mystery to me that we describe someone scatterbrained and indecisive as an *airhead*, and a frivolous conversation as *breezy*. Wind is none of those things; it is as focused as an Olympic athlete, its goal to fill a constant vacuum of rising and falling air, and doing it by bounding, bypassing, boring its way to its destination, often backflipping over cliff edges and buildings, creating currents insistent, intense, dangerous, but never wayward. Wind is a topographical empath, highly attuned to surrounding hills and nearby bodies of water, but also acted upon by bigger forces, such as the exchange of heat from the poles to the equator. I think of that sometimes, how the wind down my little runway is ultimately a traveler from tens of thousands of miles away.

. . .

There are a few final checks before I nose onto the runway to start the takeoff roll, and we call this the "run-up," though the actual running up of the engine is only one part of the procedure. The run-up is executed with care and a bit of impatience in an offset area. This space is sometimes big enough for a few aircraft at once but may consist of only a small patch clear of the runway, big enough just for you (sometimes there is no run-up area at all and you perform the sequence at the hold short line, just shy of the runway itself). Wherever the run-up area resides, it is a liminal space, in both the literal sense between the runway and the taxiway, and in the more metaphorical sense too, a transitional moment between human and bird.

It isn't just aircraft; the naturally winged have their own version of a run-up before flight. Butterflies and bees warm their engine by either flapping their wings or vibrating them at high speed to elevate their body temperature. Some types of beetles take deep breaths; scientists guess that this provides oxygen to the system, as well as adding heat. Birds have a run-up too; Canada geese may engage in head tossing and throat humming to indicate to the flock that they wish to take to the sky. Movements and sounds increase; the head moves, the white feathers of the face appear and flash; finally, wings are slowly flapped or spread to start the synapses firing. There might be vocalizations, as well as a few warm-up launches, in which the bird skims the ground only to circle back and land. These actions are most often initiated by leaders or heads of a family; a less respected youngster can try it but the flock almost certainly won't follow, and then the abashed teen must wheel back and pretend nothing has happened. As the birds lift from the ground, scientists report that the humming turns to that familiar honking (perhaps the bird version of *Nyah, nyah, last one is a rotten egg*).

It strikes me that human pilots do a version of all this when they pull on their protective flight suits, shake off any last-minute nerves, tell one another where they plan to fly, then amble slowly outside the hangar for one last look at the windsock and the traffic pattern and the wide, interminable sky.

. . .

It is here, during the run-up and right before flight, that we begin to wonder, how do we really get into the sky? What is the physics? Is there physics? It's magic, right? Even for a pilot like me who has over a thousand hours in the air, flying feels like voodoo, something sublime and supernatural.

I'm not the only one sometimes baffled. Turns out there may be no clear answer to what keeps planes aloft. As John D. Anderson, curator for aerodynamics at the Smithsonian Institution's National Air and Space Museum, told the *New York Times*, scientists disagree over the physics of flight. "Here we are,

100 years after the Wright brothers, and there are people who give different answers to this question."

When I mention this to non-pilot friends, a panicky look crosses their faces. And who can blame them? I quickly tell them that the math works out; this is what allows for upgrades to aerodynamic design. But, yes, okay, there just isn't a complete *understanding* of what those numbers are saying . . .

The panicky look remains.

There are two competing and overlapping theories. (Doesn't that reassure you—*two!*) Take the Bernoulli principle. Early wing designers took this into account when fashioning the wing's distinct shape, rounded on top and flatter on the bottom (often called an "airfoil"). This, they say, makes air rush much faster over the top of the wing than the bottom. Differing velocities, according to Bernoulli, leads to differing air pressure; the slower airspeed below the wing means high pressure, while the zipping air overhead means lower pressure.

Naturally, the higher pressure underneath wants to fill vacancies above with itself. "Lift," then, is the result of the aircraft being sort of *pushed* from below.

But Bernoulli is an incomplete explanation. Among other things, it relies on the airfoil shape to describe lift; yet planes fly upside down all the time and stay aloft. Some wings (like those of the early Wright Flyer) are even flat on both surfaces, so how does that work, for goodness' sake?

In leaps Newton's Third Law of Motion, which says that for every action there is an equal and opposite reaction ("When two bodies interact they apply forces that that are equal in magnitude and opposite in direction," says the *Encyclopaedia Britannica*). In the case of flight, air flowing over a wing drops downward at the trailing edge. The aircraft stays aloft, then, because of an equal and opposite push back upward. Or, as Wolfgang Langewiesche wrote in his seminal book *Stick and Rudder: The Explanation of the Art of Flying*, "The wing keeps the airplane up by pushing the air down." But how this air is directed down isn't fully explained by Newton, says Dr. Scott Eberhardt, a physicist and the author of *Understanding Flight*. Eberhardt credits an attraction between air molecules and the surface of the wing (called the Coandă effect) and says (again opaquely, in my opinion) that "It's really a huge amount of air pulled down from the top." Ultimately most agree, like Rod Machado, author of the popular *Private Pilot Handbook*, that the laws work together, or, as one video says rather obscurely, "they're two different ways of looking at the same thing." (I remember being taught only the Bernoulli principle when I learned to fly Cessnas in 1982.) The physics professor Rhett Allain chimes in, admitting that "with physics, it's always complicated" and explaining lift this way: "The wing crashes into the air in such a way that it pushes it down. Since forces come in pairs, pushing the air down means the air pushes up on the wing. Boom, that force is what we call lift."

Confused? Me too.

Even Einstein was stumped. He sided mostly with Bernoulli, then proceeded to design a wing that flew, according to a test pilot, with the agility of "a pregnant duck." Einstein abandoned his efforts after that, stating later that his interest in aerodynamics had been youthful folly.

Why get into that hulking airliner, then, if not all the important questions have been completely and thoroughly answered? If I can't explain how a simple experimental aircraft flies, can you trust a 450-ton 747 to take to the sky safely, with you aboard?

Despite its gray areas, flight happens. Successful new wing shapes and aircraft fuselages are being designed all the time. Smart engineers with deep knowledge of fluid dynamics are getting planes in the air, no problem, and once in the air these creations behave responsibly and predictably. As the Dreamliner pilot and author Mark Vanhoenacker assures us, an aircraft wants to fly. It is so stable in the air that "for an untrained pilot, 'Do nothing' is my first bit of counsel."

I can only advise this: uncertainty about flight should be treated much like uncertainty about love. Surely most of us don't load up on Xanax in the face of love, even as its future also promises doors that fall off without warning and collisions with obstacles unforeseen. We're nervous, sure, but excited too. It's put up tray tables, shut off phones, check your seat belt, flight attendants be seated—let's get this show on the road. And yet love adheres to no logic. There is no way to predict who or when it will strike, how that will happen, and whether it is a good idea. We know so little about love, and yet we launch ourselves enthusiastically skyward anyway.

. . .

Tailwinds portend good fortune, according to sailors and perhaps bicycle racers, but not if you're trying to get into the sky. It's a headwind that creates that needed airflow over the wing. To generate our own headwind, we call on *thrust*, or forward motion, often using an engine propeller, though in the case of a paraglider or hang glider, it starts with your own two feet, running headlong toward a steep cliff. You take flight as air starts to flow across the wing's surface; if it's a very windy day, the headwind quickly provides the needed lift, so a launch may take just one forward step, while on a no-wind day you will run for much longer.

Here's something else to remember. Newton told us that every action has an equal and opposite reaction. Fighting upward lift is downward gravity, or more specifically the weight of the aircraft. Fighting forward thrust (by the propeller, say) is the backward drag of that aircraft itself—its array of metal/canvas/aluminum parts, or even hanging legs (if you're a paraglider pilot, not from a fixed wing plane, please), all of which block air, and we call this *drag*.

Lift and weight. Thrust and drag.

"Learning to fly," says Rod Machado's *Private Pilot Handbook*, "is really learning to manage these Four Forces." Straight and level flight happens when these natural laws are perfectly balanced. So voilà, this is the simple physics (told simply too) that keep both a bird and an airliner in the sky.

Yet opposing forces don't always find graceful equilibrium. Earthbound, I am an integral part of a marriage that faces—there is no better way to say it—decreasing lift. Once soaring with ease, now the two of us are mired in drag and weight, in lack of forward motion, all tooth and claw, fighting too much. Many days are spent with strained voices, and stomping, and separating into different rooms with doors closed sharply, or in some cases silently (to outdo the other with our restraint). Mostly we engage in the sort of fighting in which you have no idea what you are fighting about. It begins on a clear afternoon that suddenly mists over and within moments we find ourselves errantly in a fog bank: that same sudden disorientation, that momentary stupefaction, that drop in the stomach as the realization sets in that things have gone wrong. Then the effort to stay straight and level, but the senses don't respond correctly: words all wrong, tone even worse, sending both of us into a spin, downward, fast, then faster.

5

Drag

Most of us have known how a relationship dissects, first almost imperceptibly and then catastrophically, like an artery. It's not that interesting, especially when you still admire, and respect, and yes, love, the other (so much more interesting when two people have betrayed and deceived, been cads or been horrors). Ours was the boring sort of devolvement, of simply growing apart. This may have been why we fought: we were clawing but clinging too. We were trying to mend, but we didn't want to mend either. We were like those knitters who knit to pass the time in DMV queues and then unwind what they've done almost dispassionately, then knit again. We were not dispassionate, though. We were angry at the knitting and at the unwinding. We didn't know what we wanted, clearly, and so we yelled, then threw up our arms in dramatic resignation, and marched into different rooms. Slowly the day came when my house no longer felt like home, but my hangar did. I would lift my hand and say *'Bye. I'm heading to the hangar.* But I didn't mean *heading,* I meant *fleeing.*

My mother, afflicted with Parkinson's, has a recurring hallucination: her house is suddenly not her house. Everything looks as it should, but it doesn't feel as it should, and so she declares, *This is not my house. It's almost my house, but not my house,* and she needs to go back to her real house, she tells us. In our rush to resolve her increasing agitation, we start, inevitably, with reason: "Why would we buy two houses that are exactly the same, Mom?" we say, dumb in our belief that we can divert this. We think common sense will simply click off this synaptic byway. It will realign this neural diphthong, this strange duplication. "Yes, why *would* you do that," she snips back, now hallucination-annoyed at our financial incompetence. "This looks like my house, but it's not my house."

Next, we try gently agreeing. We say, "Well, it's almost exactly like your house, isn't that good enough?" And often, if there are typhoons on the news, or wars unresolved, and she has the feeling that of all things, having two houses can't be so bad, she says yes, and shrugs, and we stay in that fake house until the feeling passes and she is fine again. But there are times when the house feels too alien, too hostile. Something nefarious about the mimicry agitates and she won't let it go, a dawning unease spreading to fear, and then we head for our coats and hats saying *Okay, no problem, let's go to your real house,* and we get in the car and we drive around and we get back to the house (the only house) and say a version of *Ta-da, here it is.* Invariably she is amazed at how quickly her belongings and furniture have been transferred from one house to the other and we hold our breath, hoping that this won't derail our deception, but invariably hallucinations also allow for movers who are quick and efficient and never follow up with a bill. She climbs the stairs and looks around. "I'm so glad to be home," she says.

The verbal combat in my house is not a hallucination. But increasingly I feel as my mother does: that my home is no longer my home. I still refuse to look at this head-on, just remain spooked at how what was once a haven of love and comfort has tipped into a place of anxiety and discomfort. And so I drive (flee) to my second house, stepping in with a sigh of relief. I gaze around the disheveled hangar, willy-nillied by cabinetry and camper chairs and socket sets and flight suits and oil pans. And there, in the middle, shines the little yellow gyrocopter, with its buttons that when pressed do exactly as promised, with its manageable challenges, and the certainty that my relationship with it will get better and better. Slowly I become a competent gyrocopter pilot and in some sort of weird exchange, a worse and worse wife. I excel at flying while failing slowly and inexorably at partnership, a balancing of forces that I don't fully comprehend at the time. The downward push of disappearing love. The upward push of an absorbing distraction. The forward motion of the future, the drag of the past. And here I am in the present moment, trying to make sense of it all.

6

A Short, Incomplete History of Flight

It all begins with birds.
 I'm not a formal "birdwatcher"—I can't identify calls or describe mating rituals or even match a bird with a name—but I'm engrossed, like most pilots, by birds in flight. The small ones twist and turn like trapeze artists. They approach a branch at full speed, then abruptly alight with perfect grace. They hop without fear of falling, then take off with little effort on a narrow, often moving, runway. They swirl through dense forest, never getting knocked out by a leaf or branch. No wonder the poet Mary Oliver wrote about an owl in flight this way: it "turns its face from me, and pours itself into the air."

Pours itself into the air.

"The desire to fly is an idea handed down to us by our ancestors who . . . looked enviously on the birds soaring freely through space, at full speed, above all obstacles, on the infinite highway of the air," mused Orville Wright. It's true, those of

Why Fly

us who dream of flight have always peered upward at the avian glide, beginning thousands of years ago when someone living in China cut paper and silk to a birdlike shape and invented kites, which were then flown to measure wind direction and distance during military campaigns and to signal to their armies. There are reports of prisoners tied to kites and flown from ramparts; in 1292 Marco Polo claimed to have seen a sailor bound to a large cloth frame, let loose behind a ship, then watched carefully for wind information and augurs of good or bad fortune. (For the ship. The fortune for the sailor was probably mostly bad.)

Leonardo da Vinci was renowned as a painter but he was also an inventor, and he too watched birds fly for scientific inspiration (he also hated to see birds crammed into cages and often bought them at the market just to free them). This mechanical aspect of his genius wasn't known to the world until four hundred years after his death, when, in the nineteenth century, his notebooks surfaced. Among the prophetic sketches of submarines and tanks and crossbows were studies of bird flight and drawings of flying machines, including one for an "ornithopter," which was to mechanically flap its wings and lift from the ground.

The goal was to fly like a bird, but by the eighteenth century the best anyone had done was fly like a balloon, and they did so under variously heated monstrosities that were difficult to steer and even more difficult to keep from catching on fire. In 1783 the first manned basket launched using a huge silk and paper balloon and, according to the National Ballooning Museum (yes! there is one), reached 500 feet altitude and flew for twenty-five minutes while the pilots "hand-fed fire through openings in the balloon's skirt," and perhaps prayed to any gods who might help them. Balloon attempts prior to this had often ended in conflagration, so it was with some relief that less than two weeks later another balloon successfully lifted into the air eschewing an open flame and instead using a recently discovered lighter-than-air gas called *hydrogen* (which is still very flammable).

A balloon's lift differs from bird flight in that it is reliant not on airflow but on natural laws that include hot air rising, and on Archimedes' principle, which describes an upward force equal to the weight of the fluid (air) that the balloon has displaced. Control remained rudimentary—ballast was thrown from the basket if the balloon got too low, gas was vented to land. Otherwise, steering was impossible, the pilot captive to the whims of the wind. In 1785 a balloon outfitted with a rudder fashioned after a bird tail and a hand-cranked "propeller" that flapped like a bird wing did make it across the English Channel, flown by a French inventor named Jean-Pierre Blanchard. But it was not until the early twentieth century, when dirigibles, also known as zeppelins or airships, added engine-driven propellers that allowed for directional input. Finally, controlled flight was possible for balloon-like craft.

Of course, human history is one of fits and starts. In 1982, uncontrolled flight was still alive and well when a truck driver interested in flight but with no practical experience bought forty-two sturdy weather balloons from a military surplus store, filled them with helium, and tied them to the lawn chair on which he sat. Carrying a pellet gun to shoot out balloons for descent and a CB radio for communication, as well as sandwiches, Coca-Cola, beer, and a camera, Lawrence Walters untethered the lawn chair and rose quickly to 16,000 feet, where he and his brightly colored contraption were reported by airliners flying nearby. After shooting a few balloons, "Lawn Chair Larry," as he came to be known, descended. He had been in the air forty-five minutes. He arrived back on earth only semisuccessfully: his balloons snagged on electrical wires and the chair hung there, but eventually the hapless pilot climbed down unharmed.

In the nineteenth century, flying dreamers kept at it; the more intrepid (or mad) attached feathers to their arms and jumped from high places with disastrous results. Others, like the melancholy nineteenth-century Frenchman Alphonse Pénaud, began more judiciously, using models to experiment. Riffing on earlier designs from a century before, he tensioned rubber bands to power rotor-like blades (unwittingly mimicking a Chinese toy invented a thousand years prior) that spun like a top and then took to the air. This design became an immensely popular children's knick-knack; one found its way to two young boys named Orville and Wilbur Wright, who, years later, cite it as an early inspiration for their own love of flight and thus the invention of the modern-day airplane. Pénaud never got a final aircraft design off the ground; when he was thirty years old, he approached the famed dirigible pilot and inventor Henri Giffard for support to build a human-piloted craft but was rebuffed. Aggrieved, he piled all his aeronautical diagrams and studies into a coffin, sent it to Giffard, and committed suicide.

Meanwhile, a British baronet named Sir George Cayley was also busy trying to understand aerodynamics and the possibilities of humans in the air. He eventually assembled an aircraft that looked much like a modern biplane, and in 1849 he achieved something that resembled the way a bird might fly through the air, minus arm flapping. His first pilot was a ten-year-old boy, so the term "pilot" might be generous. (This was presciently similar to a century later when the Russians won the space race by rocketing Laika the dog into orbit aboard Sputnik 2. Both situations seem patently unfair, though the ten-year-old lived, while Laika suffered a slow and terrible death in her confined cockpit.)

After that Cayley is said to have employed his butler, or perhaps his grandson—it is unclear. Whoever it was traveled 900 meters across a field and crash-landed. With all this, Cayley became the first to actively test a contraption that allowed a human to leave the ground and achieve forward motion—what we call *glide*—instead of simply dropping like a stone. While this could be considered a step forward in our quest to become airborne, it was not yet what we would consider controlled flight—the ability to leave the ground and then return to it safely, and with some sort of grace.

Around this time, the German Otto Lilienthal came onto the scene. He too wanted to fly like a bird, not like a balloon. He began as so many had before him, studying the way birds flapped their wings, then covering human arms with frames of feathers and cloth to do the same. Quickly understanding that the human body did not have the stamina to flap these wings with enough propulsive energy to stay aloft, he built models with wind-up springs that jerked articulating parts covered in feathers. Sadly, he did not get the memo that Cayley had figured out much of the physics of flight a few years before, nor had he read the paper Cayley had published in 1810 called *On Aerial Navigation*, so it was on his own that Lilienthal finally realized it wasn't just the design of a bird that mattered, there were clues to aerodynamic laws in their very behaviors. Lilienthal began to watch closely avian takeoff, flight, and landings, and he noticed, for instance, that a stork, upon seeing a human approach, might turn toward that human for its takeoff run, thus surmising that a headwind, even when it meant running toward a threat, was important. Lilienthal also realized that birds, despite their hollow bones, were not lighter than air, so flying did not depend on negligible body weight. Gravity was still in effect. So how did the beloved rooks, hawks, and storks Lilienthal peered at day after day defy that force and take to the sky, even—as the stormy petrel does over the ocean—stay there for days, weeks, months, *years* at a time with minimal effort? Lilienthal applied his knowledge of fluid dynamics and mechanics (he also invented and patented a safer steam-powered engine) and teased out the main forces governing flight, calling them *gravity, propulsion, resistance,* and *lift* (as noted above, today we call the first three *weight, thrust,* and *drag*) and concluded that forward propulsion—be it bird leg, wing flap, or propeller—was key.

Some of Lilienthal's bird flight simulators worked (one outfitted with actual pigeon wings managed to fly across two rooms), but the larger ones, tested under cover of darkness to avoid ridicule and sometimes with a small engine attached, suffered breakages, biffs, and crashes. Lilienthal ultimately changed his focus, turning his attention to simple wing shapes instead. He flew kites from the ground, then progressed to hanging from the frame by his armpits and running off a hill. He calculated airflow across cambered wings at various angles (called *angles of attack*); his final aircraft looked something like a modern-day hang glider.

Lilienthal understood aerodynamics but was always just short of consistently safe flying. Instead, after two thousand flights of varying success, in which he wobbled to the ground, crash-landed, or simply crashed, he finally managed to stay precariously aloft for as far as 250 meters (820 feet). Inevitably, though, the day came: Otto Lilienthal crashed and died.

The Wright brothers read about Lilienthal in magazines, and then a few months later they read of his death. (This "increased our interest in the subject," says Orville Wright in his book *How We Invented the Airplane.*) They subsequently wrote to the Smithsonian Institution for any information on flight and were sent a list of papers written by various obsessives with unpoetic titles like *Story of Experiments in Mechanical Flight, Problem of Flying,* and *Practical Experiments in Soaring.* By tracking down and reading other people's work, the brothers were able to skip the unsuccessful wing flapping so many had embarked on, as well as to understand that the aerodynamics had already been worked out, so it was less flight itself that was the puzzle and more stability once in the air. And so it was: the Wright brothers set about inventing the first honest-to-God controllable flying machine the world had ever seen.

According to the Weather Bureau, Kitty Hawk in North Carolina was one of the windiest places in the country. This, along with its high, soft sand dunes, made it a perfect place for test flights, the Wrights realized, and for two years they worked there (also part of the endeavor was their undersung sister, Katherine Wright, who offered insights and managed the business side of their aviation dream, overseeing finances, promotion, and sales). They studied air pressure tables and calculated wingspans. They affixed pulleys to tug the wing, increasing steadiness while in the turn (a maneuver they called "wing warping"). They assessed water tables to understand the marine screw propeller and adapted it to air currents. They manufactured their own 8-horsepower engine. The conundrums of lift, propulsion, and control had held back the development of safe, consistent flying machines, and the Wright brothers would finally solve all three.

On December 17, 1903, with Orville at the helm, simply because it was his turn, and Wilbur nearby on the ground, their fabric-covered, propeller-driven, double-winged cantilevered aircraft, appropriately named *Flyer*, took to the air and flew straight and without incident, then landed 100 feet away. (This accounts for an ongoing battle between the state where

Why Fly

the Wright brothers were born and the state where the Wright brothers finally flew. Ultimately, Ohio claimed BIRTHPLACE OF AVIATION on their automobile license plates, and North Carolina tagged themselves FIRST IN FLIGHT.) Three more successful flights followed, the final one lasting almost a minute, traveling nearly 900 feet at a speed of 30 miles per hour.

The rest, as they say, is history.

It is a long and humble through line, from kite to ornithopter to bird models to balloons to arm flapping to hang gliders to the Wright *Flyer* to B-52s to Dreamliners to today, this very morning. Any one of those inventors would be agog at my aircraft, simple as it is. It chugs happily along the ground. It gathers speed quickly on the runway. Its rotor blade, shaped like a long, thin wing, spins with the oncoming wind, generating lift. It takes off elegantly, and once in the air, its true medium, it climbs quickly and steadily. A miracle! But no, they understand. It's physics. It's design. And birds, of course, always birds.

7

Airborne

When fixed wing pilot Marion Springer first saw a gyrocopter she was not impressed. "There was no enclosure around the airframe so everything, pilot included, was just hanging out in the breeze," she writes in her memoir, *Born Free: My Life in Gyrocopters*. "The stark openness of the giro most assuredly did not convey a sense of comfort or security, at least in me. For a flying machine, there didn't seem much to it."

When I first see a gyro, I also scoff. But my friend Paul, a trike pilot for many years with a hangar next to mine, is enchanted. He sells his trike, redirecting his heart to an open cockpit rotorcraft he names Woodstock, its bright yellow color recalling the small yellow bird in the *Peanuts* comic strip.

Paul is an Englishman with an engineering mind and a dry wit. He doesn't seem the type to name a mechanical object unless truly besotted. But I'm still not sold. Then Paul mentions that he recently flew to South Lake Tahoe for the day. *South Lake*

Tahoe? I retort, half disbelieving. In a trike, with its large wing and light load, a round-trip flight to that area would be tricky; you'd have to time the journey to evade the high winds flinging themselves over the surrounding Sierra Nevada mountains during most of the lighted hours. It's different in a gyro, Paul tells me. The sleek rotor blades handle turbulence easily. You don't have to be so judicious. He adds the kicker, something that won't make sense to the non-pilot but resonates with anybody in the cockpit of a lightweight aircraft: *I can fly any time of day.* My mouth drops open.

For me, trike flying days start before sunrise and definitively end at 10:30 A.M. They demand assiduous attention to outwit the turbulence that develops by late morning. This includes scrutiny of weather sites the preceding day and a sleepy call from bed before dawn to the airport's automated weather box searching for clues, and finally an hour's drive to the hangar trying to discern the amount of sway in the trees and bushes along the dark roadside. If the morning is a bust for sure—fog is often an issue—I don't even start the drive, instead hoping for a flight in the waning evening light when the air is supposed to be calm. All in all, the possibility of avoiding much of this divination and wind witching sparks a fleeting, then less fleeting, thought: *Perhaps I should fly a gyrocopter.*

Gyros were invented in 1923 by Juan de la Cierva, who named his aircraft *autogiro*. The *auto* referred to the fact that the rotors spin by themselves with the incoming wind; *giro* is Greek for "spiral." There was a motor-driven propeller at the back used for thrust, and a spindly frame in which the pilot would sit; it looked much like the gyro Marion Springer laid her eyes on forty years later.

Springer resisted the gyro at first; it was her husband, Docko, who, bored with the aircraft they owned, wanted what he called more "pizzazz" in his flying life. It was the 1960s and the *autogiro* was still a rudimentary affair, delivered as a jumble of parts to the hopeful pilot who would then assemble and test the flying machine it would become. You could buy factory-made blades, but they were expensive, so more likely you would hone them yourself from spruce and mahogany and glue. In addition, there were no gyro flight instructors, so builders like the Springers would learn using a step-by-step booklet that the Bensen Aircraft Company, maker of these parts, also provided.

"As I got more involved in the construction of the gyro, I started to feel a little bit friendlier toward the machine," Marion writes. Soon enough, she was curious about flying it. With the Bensen finally assembled, she pored over the flight instruction booklet. Learning to fly a gyro using only a written manual is mindboggling to me: Where was the keen-eyed instructor in the next seat who would gently (or not so gently) remind of correct technique, and grab the controls if things got hairy? Nowhere. Certified teachers did not exist for this aircraft, and the solo seat would have precluded one anyway. Instead, the new pilot was responsible for herself once in flight, much like the long string of enthusiasts before her, like Lilienthal and the Wright brothers. Springer writes that Docko wisely restrained her at every turn, making sure she had mastered each incremental step before proceeding to the next skill. Many early gyro pilots, she notes, did not have this voice of reason nearby, and they did not survive their own instruction.

When I begin my own lessons a full sixty years after the Springers, there are still not many gyro teachers. I travel first to Arizona. As I near full certification I start casting about for a gyro to buy into; pilots routinely partner up to share the costs of an aircraft, which accrue quickly and mercilessly (there are also flying clubs, whose members have access to multiple aircraft). My parameters are simple: an open cockpit, and a hangar within a reasonable drive of my home. But the search is daunting. There are so few gyro pilots to begin with, and those who exist mostly enjoy enclosed flight.

Providence steps in. Paul's old partner no longer wants to fly; am I interested, he asks? God bless the man, believing in this rotorcraft beginner. In many ways we are different pilots: I am someone who doesn't care about turbocharge, or the 115 horsepower, or the trick avionics he has so lovingly assembled. A panel with every conceivable gauge? Shrug, yawn. Open cockpit? Good flying feel? A must.

While I am certified to make certain repairs, I find no joy in the process, easily flummoxed by an odd sound or indicator light or errant drip. Paul, on the other hand, is a genius in the face of all things that whir and click and send electrical currents to and fro. In the future we soon have together, it isn't uncommon for Woodstock to have a small problem and the next day Paul to call me to say he's gone ahead and repaired it, no need to hire somebody. He pondered it all night, he says with Sherlockian intensity, then reels off a series of sentences in what must be a foreign language to describe his diagnosis and the ensuing fix. I thank my lucky stars to have a partner (and friend) in Paul, who keeps Woodstock in tip-top shape, while I offer only regular payment, a clean hangar, a perpetual shine on our yellow aircraft, and a similar enthusiasm for flight itself, someone who hears *South Lake Tahoe, any time of day*, and thinks *Yes*.

Paul's stipulation to partnership is that I learn to fly Woodstock's make and model, a Magni M-16, and that I get the nod from an instructor he respects. I travel to Texas to fly with Dayton, a young cowboy-looking pilot prone to dad jokes (though he isn't yet a dad). Dayton is endlessly patient and not easily ruffled by my wavering figure eights and bumpy landings, smoothing them out with just a few well-spaced pointers. When I do manage something with semicompetence, he drawls out praise. One day he takes the controls: he lands, but instead of touching down, remains just inches off the ground, still flying. He then "air-taxis" a left turn off the runway, right turn on the taxiway, left turn again across the tarmac, left once more, and finally settles the wheels onto pavement near his hangar. *This is what can be done, pipsqueak*, he seems to be saying, but nicely. He isn't showing off, just underscoring the gyro's potential and my own future in it. When Dayton gives the okay to Paul that I can be trusted with Woodstock's suspension and general health, I feel not just ready, but qualified.

Docko and Marion could not initially afford an engine, so they decided to fly their new aircraft as a gyroglider. This meant first learning to "kite" it by tying it to a stationary object on the ground with a 60-foot rope, spinning up the overhead rotor by hand, and hoping the stiff wind was enough to send the gyro and pilot aloft. All this took patience and the right weather conditions. That first time, on an ocean bluff with a curious crowd of strangers gathered around, it was hours before Springer found herself finally airborne; and stunned. "Bobbing up and down on the wind, moving side to side, then back to center, touching down, then lifting off again," she writes, "there was exhilaration, but there was also something else, a sense that this was what I had been waiting for all my life. Such a feeling of completeness came over me . . . I love my little airplane, but it doesn't compare with this. The gyro is so wonderful, so free, so free."

I may add here, boastfully perhaps, that many experienced pilots feel this way. Dayton flies a multitude of different aircraft, including jets, and still proclaims the poky, unadorned gyro his favorite.

Springer loved the gyro for its elegant turns, its bare-minimum feel—both cutting horse and asteroid at once. She admired, too, how safe it would prove to be: even if its engine failed, the rotors continued to spin; it touched down at slow speeds in tight spaces; and though it did not hover like the helicopter it resembles, it also will not stall. This last factor continues to amaze those of us accustomed to an airfoil that cannot go below a certain airspeed lest it jerk suddenly sideways and begin to fall, no longer flying. The stall is one of the most dreaded scenarios, one from which pilots incessantly practice efficient recovery. Airspeed (not groundspeed!) is vital for keeping a plane from stalling, and woe be to you if you fly too slow too close to the ground. Not so in a gyro. I routinely slow it to a standstill in the air just to feel it drop vertically, still flying but unable to maintain altitude, just as Springer surely did so many years ago. I do this because it is a quick way to descend in, say, a narrow canyon. But mostly I do it to be amazed.

Soon the Springers graduated to towing each other aloft using a pickup truck and an abandoned military runway. "We would start out thinking we would spend two or three hours practicing and would end up there all day," she writes. "Our children were practically abandoned." Ultimately the Bensen gained an engine, and then finally an extra seat in which students could be instructed by the first female gyro instructor ever, Marion Springer herself. Springer flew until her mideighties. "Give me a gyro, a tank of gas, and time to fly, and I was in heaven. Throw in a little wind . . . who could ask for anything more?"

The naturalist, author, and pilot Diane Ackerman says of flying: "It isn't that I find danger ennobling, or that I require cheap excitation to cure the dullness of routine. But I do like the moment, central to danger and to some sports, when you become so thoroughly concerned with acting deftly in order to be safe that only *reaction* is possible, not analysis. You shed the centuries and feel creatural." That is what I seek these days—my more elemental self. The creatural in me.

Ironically, I also have that most human of needs, to feel a little in control, to step off the foundation that is crumbling under me onto something firmer. Could I hold both at once, the creatural and the one that makes choices, summons will, says *no*, says *yes*, says *I will think about it*?

"The pilot seat is of the few places on earth where one's life is truly one's own," Ackerman writes, confirming I can be primal and the Decider at once. I can find footing in that most unfooting and ethereal of places: the sky. Bumble in daily life, then, but here, about to take off, the procedure is so clear. The gyro engine has been revved, the ignition tested. The gauges are in the green, the numbers are right. The rotor blades have been spun up and now they blaze above me, shaking the tiny fuselage in which I'm seated, insisting that the takeoff roll begin. I have been assiduously monitoring the radio but I glance upward anyway, clocking any aircraft in the pattern, any birds in my way. The hawk is there looking bored; meanwhile, this human is wide-eyed and tense-necked with anticipation. I taxi forward. I hold short of the runway. These are my final moments earthbound. I glance around once more, then key the mic, already in thrall of the waiting sky.

PART 4

TAKEOFF

More than anything else, Jonathan Livingston Seagull loved to fly.

RICHARD BACH, *JONATHAN LIVINGSTON SEAGULL*

8

Lift

When the gyrocopter breaks past that final earthly barrier—a simple painted hold short line—and onto the runway, the pilot's head is still "on a swivel," as instructors like to say. She must be sure no aircraft is on final approach, be convinced no errant birds flit about, confirm that any landing plane has exited the runway. If there's a passenger in the back seat he's been told to keep the cockpit "sterile"—which doesn't mean an antiseptic wipe-down or a blue gown, but simply that the linked headsets remain quiet for now, clean of any comments or questions. This is because the takeoff is the most dangerous of the flying stages. The pilot brain can have no distractions—it must shunt important information to the appendages that work the rudder and the stick and remind the eyes to keep a peripheral glance on the instruments; this is much like the body on alert redirecting the blood to the vital organs, meaning that chatter by a passenger is the equivalent of sending hemoglobin to, say, the elbow.

Anyway, descriptors can't capture the anticipation or that slight tremor inside. So why speak? No words are adequate for this changing state of matter. Like liquids to gases or solids to liquids, from melting to freezing to vaporizing, so we soon go from Sapien to Avian.

The engine now roars to full power. Wheels kick and spin; the runway centerline gallops beneath. As forward speed increases, this line unfurls from broken white into one long dancer's ribbon. Imperceptibly at first, then with more insistence, the nose begins to lift. The mains continue to argue that earthbound is the natural state even as the rotor begs to differ. Soon there is buoyancy, but gravity and lift still bicker. Barring a flat tire, a sudden swooping bird, the smell of smoke, a disconcerting sound, or an instrument that snaps suddenly into the red, it is lift that will prevail. (If any of the former happens, the alert pilot slams the throttle shut and pushes down the nose, and the battle swings to gravity again.) At a certain airspeed, all wheels leave the tarmac. And then there it is.

Flight.

This is lightness felt as promise, as hope, as possibility.

But of course, a takeoff is also a leaving.

It is easy to be stupefied by this freeing, to be stunned by float. But there is no time to wax poetic: the moment still demands attention. Lift at this height is precarious. Not because of the air, but because of the ground. Takeoff is a vengeful Greek god; eager for any excuse to throw lightning bolts, it has little forgiveness. This is why even as Newton and Bernoulli dutifully step in, I keep the gyro close to the ground. I can feel the insistence of lift, but I stay just inches from the asphalt, ensuring that the lift is true, that the blade is spinning fast, that there is no errant *pop, bang, thwack,* or *schwiiiing*—all amusing sounds when written in bubble script on the page of a superhero comic book, but dreaded for the lowly mortal pilot. When my airspeed is high enough, only then do I nudge the nose upward. There is the odd sensation of the ground falling away, not of me rising from it. Earth molts on all sides, streaks of color and form that slant backward while white-blue takes up the windshield.

I am flying.

The author and pilot Mark Vanhoenacker lauds landings more than takeoffs (he lauds them so much he wrote a short book called *How to Land a Plane*). It's more challenging, he says, and points out that "no one has to take off, after all." And if we do take off (how can we resist, really?), we must eventually land. I will grant that the skill it takes to touch back down is greater than any other in flight. Yet takeoffs are more critical. During landing, if an engine sputters and dies on final approach, or a gauge shoots into the red on the downwind leg, the runway is (should be) within reach. On takeoff this not true: in the preliminary few moments of a gyrocopter's flight, the 180-degree turn back to the airport is impossible, even for my nimble aircraft.

Landlubbers think of the ground as safe and the air as dangerous, but pilots know otherwise: the dreaded engine-out that occurs at a thousand feet is hair-raising, but at 200 feet it is likely to be deadly. High altitude allows precious time to fix the sudden problem, prepare for an emergency landing. At low altitude that needed time has been halved, or sliced into one fourth, one hundredth. For this reason, I have already mentally registered the opening off to the right if something goes wrong. But will it work? What of that tree, those wires, these newly built houses, that rolling golf cart in the middle of a tilting green? The words my brain is reciting in those first moments of flight would horrify a passenger if heard out loud—*If it all goes to shit, I could land there, or there, now there, and there.*

Why Fly

The hope is to make the emergency landing dead ahead, and indeed stories of early flight are littered with planes forced down into fields, whose pilots emerge from the mud slapping their flying breeches with just a shake of the head, then wield a wrench to fix the problem and soon take off again. But with the encroachment of houses and malls and crowded roadways on even the smallest of airports, this open space has disappeared, and with it many of our options if anything untoward happens on takeoff.

So we keep our mind focused on worst case scenarios. So we are awash in a bleak mindset; we act as if disaster will strike at any moment. Disaster is unlikely, but we must be prepared for the unlikely, so positivity and smiles are tucked away and brought out like pretzel snacks only at sufficient altitude.

Finally, I glance at my altimeter: 500 feet. Now I can relax, sure that if anything happens my options are better, maybe even pretty good. Out comes the positivity. Out comes the smile. Out comes the fullness of the sky.

9

Gliders

The term shouldn't be *fall in love*, with its banana peel imagery, its sense of pratfall and clumsiness. We should *take off in love*. Love and takeoffs have so much in common: the heady feeling of promise, the acceleration, the sudden leap into weightlessness, even the physical drop of the stomach. These are beginnings, a trajectory launched. Ahead is potential, flight of body and mind.

Love is dangerous, as is the takeoff. One part of the human brain brims with excitement but the other part knows well the potential mishaps that await and is prepared to abort. Certainly for the first few seconds (weeks, months) we look for the signs to settle back onto the runway, taxi, park, end the flight. But these are peripheral glances, obligatory eye movements, assurances to friends and advice columnists that we have our wits about us. Mostly we fling ourselves upward. Sometimes we are propelled by the engine of our own will, the military jet jumping into the sky after the target. Sometimes it feels as if we are swept along by the beloved, pulled upward by something not of our own conscious accord. Here we are the sailplane, towed by another, but willingly, and once in the sky we become more truly ourselves.

When I first met my future wife, I wanted to be all jet, but I was without doubt mostly sailplane, resting at an angle while parked, tipped on one wing in a way that can remind of awkward adolescence. Add to that the sailplane's disproportions, from a huge ape index to a gangly torso, not to mention a pudgy-cheeked glass canopy over the cockpit, and it all adds up to a teen leaning against a wall trying to look like she belongs. On the outside I was no teen, I was a forty-two-year-old woman. But inside I was burbling with nerves, prewriting whimsical texts on a computer, changing clothes a dozen times before a date. When she turned to me, when she spoke, when she laughed, sometimes I didn't know where to put my feet, or what to say.

But those first few months, I posture jetness anyway. I pretend great speed, with turning angles that wow, all throttle and afterburners. I welcome the havoc of pheromones, which rule without consideration to how it all pertains to actual partnering, that building of a shared life. It is a weird evolutionary adaptation, good sex as the foundation for a future union. Doesn't each demand the opposite talents? The first fetishizes spontaneity, intermittent pacing, good communication (but not processing—definitely no processing), the right chemistry, and a complete immersion in the now; meanwhile, the latter can't always wait for "when it feels right" but relies on prearranged times and endlessly discussed agreements and multitasks past, present, and future, cherishes predictability, and of course entails way too much processing. I remember the jet months fondly, but it is when we decided to seriously give it a go that I became truly happy and allowed my real self to step forward. Hello sailplane, awkward while on land, transformed in the air, a sleek, slender thing specially conjured for flight. All it needs is what most of us need at various times: a little help getting airborne.

To fly anything without an engine you must be part strategist, part aeromancer, a diviner of weather and terrain. Luckily your shimmering arrow is blessed with the highest of efficiency in flight, an elegance we measure as *glide ratio*. Colloquially, this is the term for how far forward the (unpowered) wing can fly in calm air until it must finally land. An advanced paraglider—that simple contraption of fabric wing attached to a harness in which dangles an intrepid human—has a glide ratio of around 10:1; a top sailplane's may be as high as 60:1, traveling sixty kilometers forward for every one kilometer of descent. There is time, then, to make decisions, to find altitude or a landing zone, but glider pilots learn quickly that time is fleeting and it's best to think several moves ahead, like a chess player. Commitments are taken seriously; there is no throttle to hammer on when you need altitude, only the invisible promise of upward-pushing wind. Decide on a landing spot, and as you near it there are no second chances.

Despite these challenges, the sailplane finds its true calling after takeoff. Airborne, it is contemplative thought given form. It is wisps of fog. It is a light hum against a sparkling sky.

The sailplane is just one of the designs under the category of *glider*, which encompasses all piloted aircraft without engines, from paragliders and hang gliders to the space shuttle. There are even military gliders, beefy, hulking creatures big enough to hold supplies and troops yet built to belly flop and plow across rough, open fields too small and inhospitable for regular aircraft.

These four-ton behemoths were used often during World War II. They were dragged from earth by powered planes, then slung toward makeshift landing zones, sometimes deep within enemy territory. They did not soar upward on puffs of wind like the elegant sailplane, did not carve languid circles like hawks. When freed from the towline these gliders dropped fully loaded at 400 feet per minute. For this reason, they were let loose close to their intended destination, allowing pilots little time to pick a touchdown point, then come to a full stop within an amazingly short 600 feet or less, landing gear and fuselage often torn up by ruts and brush and stones along the way. (Many of the descriptions I read called the touchdowns not "landings" but "crash landings.") Gliders came in flocks, like birds. In this way the military kept their forces together, along with its necessary heavy armaments (as opposed to paratroopers and parachuted equipment, which would be dispersed over a wide area). If all went well, thirteen soldiers would quickly disembark, or one tank would drive out of its hold. Those lucky gliders that were fixable or intact were loaded up with the wounded to fly out again. But what was the new takeoff strategy? The gliders needed that powered plane to get them airborne once more.

During World War II, the solution came once again from the trusty U.S. Postal Service (the entity responsible for the mighty checklist), which had been snagging mailbags from the ground for years, using a hook and a low-altitude pass. But what worked for a satchel in a rural town didn't necessarily translate into grabbing a glider weighing as much as 9,000 pounds, loaded with the desperate and dying, and javelining it into the sky. What was needed was what was eventually concocted: a powerful aircraft (for the United States this was often a C-47 Dakota) outfitted with a skilled pilot and a system of brakes and pulleys that dampened the shock of the initial catch. This returning towplane flew below the tree line trailing a hook that snagged an awaiting rope suspended between two poles. In this way the glider was picked up "by the scruff of the neck," as one excitable British newscaster described it (though it was more like being grabbed by your nose ring), to become, in just six seconds, safely airborne.

The glider's takeoff was a nail-biting procedure, dependent on the power of the towplane and the skill of its pilot, and all manner of takeoff disasters could happen. The snatch itself was relatively gentle, but the towline could snap at low altitude. The towplane could lose an engine or encounter such bad weather en route that the gliders (sometimes they towed two behind them) would begin to dip and whip and pull, a demon on its heels. The crew of the towplane then faced a gut-wrenching decision: they would have to detach the gliders if they were to save themselves. This might happen over an ocean or in the dark of night, in which case the gliders and the humans inside stood little chance. Not to mention enemy fire from the ground, which could shred the glider's canvas-covered fuselage or bring down the towplane and the glider with it. Despite the dangers, gliders were part of almost every military campaign from 1943 onward. All told, six thousand soldiers became glider pilots.

Gliders gain altitude when wind is diverted from its horizontal flow by, say, a mountaintop or a ridge. Air also travels upward when it is heated, rising in columns called *thermals*. Birds are excellent at flying in thermals: they use these natural elevators to gain altitude without extraneous wing flapping, and in doing so they save valuable calories. You see them circling the upsurge like children at play, and when they reach its zenith, where the hot air meets a cooler layer and stops rising, they simply glide to the next ascending cushion.

Thermals were not well understood by glider pilots until the 1930s, when American and European aviators traveled to South America to fly these rumored wind currents. Thermals are invisible, but the glider pilots noted that they were topped by cumulus clouds, as the lower temperatures at higher altitudes condensed the air. They also observed how well the local vultures understood these heated upwellings. The glider pilots couldn't help themselves: they decided to bring a few of these vultures back to Europe. Watching the vultures navigate European wind currents could further edify, was the thinking. But the journey home by train and boat was long and arduous; inevitably some of the birds died. Then, once at the famed German gliding school, the ones that survived refused to leave their cages, much less fly. It was an odd, foreboding sign. Did it take only a few weeks for a bird to forget the sky? Are cages more secure than freedom? Were they simply depressed, or temporarily shell-shocked? Even when they were finally herded from their box, they remained in their old-woman hunch in the corner of the flying school's garden, scaring the maids. No amount of coaxing or threat induced them to take to the air; they flapped their wings only as weapons against an advancing stick or arm. By the third day, one had disappeared. Later it was seen waddling along the road toward Heidelberg. The other two were given to the Berlin zoo, where they were shoved into new cages.

I think of those birds sometimes. I wonder whether they ever dreamed of circling their bright Argentinian sky. And it puzzles me that they could not, or would not, fly. Were they refusing another sort of captivity, flight under the auspices of someone else's demands? Perhaps the answer is less gallant. Circumstances change, and it is so easy to forget who we are. Our essential spirit flees, hides, or is crushed. We waddle, defeated, bereft, through this new reality. Heaven is wide and blue above us, but we just can't see it anymore.

10

Migration

The sky opens and closes in gradations, a louver pulled up and down by a languid arm in a valium-slow reveal. We claim to notice the way nightfall drops, usually in our peripheral vision while driving home from work; yet most days, the sun slides away before we know it. Suddenly it is evening.

It is the pilot with a certain certification (sport pilot) who watches closely. She sees every sequential shading, knows that real night starts when the sun hits six degrees below the horizon and the light/dark balance is just so, formalized by the FAA as a half hour after sunset. This is because sport pilots are barred from night flight and so we are often found racing across the sky in this liminal space between light and dark called "civil twilight," desperate to land at the airport on time and stay within legal flying requirements.

Dawn is also slippery. Yet it has the same definitive stages if you want to look, as I do, there outside my hangar at astronomical twilight, technically that time when the sun is still 18 degrees below the horizon and the stars are not yet washed from the sky. I step out again around nautical twilight, the sun now 12 degrees below me, enough light to see the dim outline of, say, a boat on the water. At civil twilight, the sun 6 degrees away, the sky is an upward-melting Creamsicle and I am pushing my trike out onto the tarmac. The dawn chorus begins, birds singing forth the coming day, and only the soft clunk of my wheels invades, like a drum keeping time. For a moment there is nothing but this fragile truce between light and sound and temperature and living creatures, everything harmonic. Then all is interrupted by the sudden spit and jarring thrum of my engine, the blink of my navigation lights, the whole bulky contraption lumbering toward the waiting runway.

Which is why it was an unlikely, possibly crazy, idea when a man named Bill Lishman truly believed he could hoodwink birds into believing he was one of them. Lishman was a sculptor who had taught himself to fly in the early days of hang gliding, using a bi-wing contraption called the Easy Riser, which he launched at a gallop and then hung precariously from by his armpits. By 1985, Lishman had fashioned himself a rudimentary version of my own trike. He'd welded a seat to wheels, used bungee cords as shocks, added a two-stroke engine and a propeller, and topped it off with the trusty Easy Riser. The result looked more like a recumbent bicycle left under an awning than an aircraft. Lishman began to fly it regularly.

During one excursion over the barns and fields of his Canadian home, Lishman found himself joined by a flock of ducks, and the moment was akin to a religious conversion. He was not just flying like a bird; he was flying among them. He decided to raise Canada geese to be flight partners, banking that they would follow him and his homebuilt because of their instinct to "imprint." This meant that they attached to the first living being they see after they hatch, which would be, not adult geese parents, but Lishman. He documents his journey in a short film called *C'mon Geese*. Sometime in the 1990s my father managed to copy this tale from the television using the old method of VCR machine and tape and then gifted the video to me. On it a grown white man with a bushy beard and curly hair repeatedly dashes through a meadow like an oversized leprechaun, goslings trailing behind in a bobbing, clumsy, enthusiastic mob. As he runs, he exhorts "C'mon geese!" over and over while playing the endless whine of an ultralight engine on a tape recorder that dangles from one hand and the geese follow like excited kindergartners.

My father and I watched this tape multiple times, loving the zany evangelism of this human and his repeated incantation of *C'mon geese*, which we sometimes incorporated into our own conversations. As hoped, Lishman's brood eventually dashes after the ultralight itself as it taxis across the same meadow. Finally, their wings strong enough, the geese begin to lift from the ground, and so does the ultralight; eventually Lishman takes them on a glorious first flight across the sky, the ultralight an elegant avian silhouette, the geese trailing like fairy dust. It's hard not to be moved by the scene, bird and man in synchrony. At the same time, there is an aspect of cruelty to orphaning and then tricking young birds just for one's own enjoyment. Lishman may have thought so too, because he decided to put this flying to better use. In 1994 he founded Operation Migration, using trikes to reintroduce endangered birds to habitat in which they once had thrived but from which they had long since disappeared.

Among Operation Migration's first efforts was familiarizing the almost extinct American whooping crane with its old flyway.

Crane scientists decided to raise chicks who would be tended to only by humans in white, vaguely birdlike costumes. They wore veils over their faces and crane puppets on one hand; visages and voices were banned in the hopes that these puppet-fed babies would believe that they were wild birds living wild-birdy lives. When the time came, the young birds would be taught a viable migration route using Lishman's ultralight. In 2001, trike pilots donned the birdy costumes, blasted whooping crane calls from speakers on rear axles, and led the first young brood upward and eventually across the country from Wisconsin to Florida. It was a triumphant reenactment of the old migration path, which the whooping cranes would then teach to their own chicks, reviving their population and their essential selves.

Or that was the idea. In his book *Wild Ones*, the writer Jon Mooallem captures both the beauty and the quixotic nature of the effort, which was in constant thrall to bad weather, human conflict, unclear visions, and bird whim. Also looming in the background was the inexorable march of climate change, as well as the unstoppable spread of more houses, golf courses, pollution, people. "It is heroism in the Sisyphean sense, just as all conservation may be . . . It requires rallying the will to build something that the future is likely to erase."

But a pilot who has the chance to fly among birds will cling to hope past all reason. Operation Migration co-founder Joe Duff, who kept shepherding the whooping cranes long after Lishman stepped back, seemed to have felt he too owed something to the birds. "The creatures that taught us the art of flying are now being helped by the aircraft they helped design," he tells Mooallem.

The whooping cranes certainly needed the aid of those breeding sanctuaries to bounce back from their once dismal population numbers. However, they did not necessarily need to migrate. But Operation Migration and its raggedy flock of scientists, conservationists, nature preserve volunteers, bureaucrats, citizens, and pilots believed that in order to restore the birds not just to the landscape, but to their own inner wildness, migration was essential. Yet, Moollem wonders, can a bird these days really become "wild"? And how was such authenticity to be gauged? By mimicking the bird's past, it seemed: reenacting old routes, avoiding human contact. But these requirements surely meant that Operation Migration's task was impossible. Human influence was everywhere now. And what were the implications of rebooting an instinct last used more than a hundred years earlier and then sending it out over a changed landscape, one striped with power lines, partitioned by highways, sprinkled with pesticides and microplastics, blocked by skyscrapers, drained of its bogs, devoid of open space? It seemed akin to giving someone a piece of flint and an arrowhead and dropping her into Manhattan. Indeed, the migrating cranes were easily distracted by everything from effluent ponds to backyard bird feeders, the modern-day equivalents of wetlands and feeding grounds.

And yet we grope toward this ideal of "wild." Mooallem sees the irony and writes with a combination of admiration and bafflement at the "unfathomable force inside us that had once nearly destroyed the bird and was now beating just as uncontrollably in the cockpit in front of the flock." My own guess is that humans, and especially those who become pilots, feel bereft of something that they then press onto, say, endangered birds, like parents who once played a team sport and, trying to recapture what they had, push their kids to become even better than they, yelling maniacally from the sidelines, cursing coaches, driving to and fro for games. Certainly I, too, have wished to fly among birds; if I wasn't so paranoid about their striking my overhead rotor, I would venture much closer to this sublime air ballet, to these whirling, gliding, diving forms. Instead I keep a safe distance, but still I watch them hungrily, something ancient tugging inside me.

Here in the United States, the trike, with its slow speeds and open cockpit, was deemed perfect for migratory flight; meanwhile, in Europe, bird enthusiasts decided on the motored paraglider, called a *paramotor*, similarly languid and avian. Since 2004, the paramotor pilot and biologist Johannes Fritz has led northern bald ibis flocks across the landscape their ancestors once freely inhabited. The actual migration route is a continuing guess; the birds became extinct from the area four centuries ago and left little historical record (they do taste very good, though, according to one sixteenth-century naturalist). The first class of paramotor-following ibis successfully taught their offspring the migratory path Fritz had picked, from Germany to Tuscany. Climate change soon interfered, however. Lulled by longer, warmer autumns, some ibis began leaving for their southern homes later than advisable and perished in winter storms over the Alps (forty-two birds died there in 2022). It was an errant ibis named Ingrid who picked a different, longer route on his own (birds are named before their gender is determined, notes the journalist Nick Paumgarten in his *New Yorker* article on the migration effort) that avoided the Alps and Tuscany altogether and wound instead toward southern Spain via France and the Mediterranean. Fritz decided to follow. He later learned that ibis fossils had been discovered in Gibraltar and near Valencia. Had Ingrid tapped into a memory lodged in his DNA, unburying the route? This amazed Fritz. "Ingrid was the first to revive this tradition after four hundred years. This is incredible, no?"

Like the whooping cranes, these northern bald ibis are separated from their bird parents before hatching and raised by foster moms, who are the only persons ever to interact with the birds. This is true even during migration, which requires lots of milling, driving, piloting, food preparing people, all instructed to stay far away from the feathered main attraction. But the Europeans tending to the ibis have shed the earnest bird costuming, instead raising the chicks to respond to the color yellow. Only the foster moms can sport yellow, and the paragliding chute that flutters above during the migration is also yellow; no crew member is allowed to wear the hue.

There are differences beyond the sartorial; the German foster moms also eschew the birdy pantomime of their American counterparts. They show their human face, talk and sing in their human voice, and even read the Harry Potter series aloud to their charges during the down times. In the paramotor, they sit behind the pilot and coax the flock in human words through a bullhorn. The Europeans, it seems, do not dream of a truly wild bird, just one that will survive a modern world. Fritz tells Paumgarten, "We need to save the animals in a way that enables them to live with us." And when he says "us" he surely means also all that we leave in our wake, that devastation wreaked on the land and air and the changing, bird-killing weather.

Will it work? There is something harebrained about these endeavors, but also romantic. "It's the beauty of humans trying to fix a larger beauty we broke," Mooallem writes. Certainly, from the moment Lishman lures his Canada geese into the air and gets a closeup view of bird flight, he is smitten. "I can see the muscles move in the back and the movement of each feather. I notice how the head stays still while all the rest of the body is moving. When they get tired, they open their mouth," he marvels in his film's voiceover, a geek astounded by flight. Of landings, he becomes worshipful. "They do these tumbling maneuvers, and what they're doing is they're losing altitude without gaining speed. They can pull one wing in and flip sideways or upside down, then pull out ten feet down." Ultimately, he dares conclude: "When the air is still, we are just like one big organism in the sky."

As a pilot I know how open cockpit flight provokes a feeling that passes for wildness, something ginned up by the pummeling of wind and sun and too-cold temperatures. It is that "creatural" that Ackerman lauded when she first began to fly and learned to think less, react more. Landing with hair that sticks out at all angles and sunburnt cheeks and red eyes, I certainly look untamed. But I am mistaking my outer dishevelment for a more decisive inner freedom that is harder to earn; I have instead just found precious distance from civilization for a few hours and a unique connection to nature. It's a valuable and life-altering distance and connection, but it can't be proclaimed as wild. And yet we hope for more from birds, pushing them to go forth into our complex world of parking lots and wind turbines encoded with survival instincts that recall a completely different, and simpler, time.

When the news anchor Hugh Downs first interviewed Bill Lishman about Operation Migration and its whooping crane journeys, he gushed, "I think this is the most beautiful story that we've had on *20/20* in its fifteen years." His co-host, Barbara Walters, was equally entranced. "Ah, if we could all fly," she said, rendered wistful and bright-eyed, like the rest of us, at the thought of humans and birds winging side by side across the open sky.

II

The Pioneers

What of those other pivotal moments in life—these takeoffs that determine your trajectory, your access to a view? How did I become a pilot in the first place? Certainly, I was obsessed with adventure tales when I was young. I devoured books about exploits both real and imaginary, and each month sat cross-legged on the living room floor poring over those *National Geographic* magazines that arrived in our mailbox. I gaped at the dazzling photos that accompanied stories of men who slogged to the poles, or who rowed alone across the Pacific. These were oddball inventors, gallant anthropologists, and barrel-chested marine biologists, but the only one I found who in any way resembled me was the pilot Amelia Earhart.

Turns out there were other female adventurers at the time, and in the centuries before—cyclists, mountain climbers, sailors, scuba divers. But the media rarely, if ever, covered them, so all over the world girls like me thought that women didn't

Why Fly

venture outside with the same chutzpah and joy and curiosity and hell-bent bravery as men. You will be surprised to learn, as I was, that many intrepid female pilots existed; Harriet Quimby was the first woman to get a pilot's license, in 1911, and others quickly followed. And why didn't I ever come across the inimitable Bessie Coleman, who once held fans spellbound with her loops and hammerheads and rolls? She was a contemporary of Earhart's, learned to fly at almost the same time (1920), and also had many notable firsts to her name. Coleman, or Queen Bess, as she was known, was arguably as brave (or braver!), as interesting (or more!), and a better pilot, with a wide variety of skills that included aerobatics. And yet it wasn't until the astronaut Mae Jamison went to space in 1992 with a photo of Coleman that her name and legacy became familiar to me.

The reasons Queen Bess is so much less well known is simple: she was Black. She was wildly famous to all Americans in her day, but history picked Amelia Earhart, someone with a pixie haircut, a diffident smile, a girl-next-door vibe, and white skin. It was Earhart who was to be the one "girl flier" enshrined in all the textbooks I read in school. I'm not trying to take anything away from Earhart. She worked hard to earn her pilot's license; she was not born into money (though she eventually married the publishing magnate George Putnam); she struggled not just financially but also against doubt and malice on the part of male pilots and non-pilots alike, as well as a savage press who relentlessly insinuated (or outright declared) that women were too fragile and foolish to command a flying machine. Every mishap in the unreliable aircraft of the day by a female pilot was proof that she was unfit to fly; meanwhile, men were killing themselves right and left, yet were anointed brave pioneers.

Earhart legitimately won her laurels flying unworthy planes and surviving close calls and crashes because of them (she even flew an early version of my gyrocopter across the country in 1931, becoming only the second person to do so). Her fame solidified when she became the second person to fly across the Atlantic solo, five years after Charles Lindbergh, and the first woman to do so (though other women had bravely tried). During the international crossing, Earhart encountered storms, failing instruments, a fuel leak into the cockpit, and a buildup of ice on the wings—all terrifying for any pilot at night over an ocean with nowhere to land. Certainly, Earhart was my own guiding beacon—knowing that a woman had excelled at piloting planes was key to my own flying journey.

But Coleman arguably showed more American gumption, by getting a pilot's license despite the almost impassable obstacles in the way of anyone who was Black and poor, not to mention female. She knew of no role models that looked like her, except perhaps the American pilot Eugene Bullard, who fought for the French in World War 1, receiving medals for his bravery. Coleman had to travel to France for flying lessons, since no American aviator would teach her, a Black person. The pursuit was not just arduous and expensive—she eventually sought sponsorship from local businesses (a major backer was the Black newspaper, *The Defender*)—but Coleman would be taking her flying lessons *in French*. When she returned to her home country with pilot's certificate in hand—the first Black woman in the world to do so, and as a biracial woman, also the first Native American woman—still no American would teach her the aerobatics that could earn her a living on the "barnstorming" circuit, performing above small towns, county fairs, and exhibitions.

Why Fly

She returned to France to learn the barrel rolls, hammerheads, loops, and figure eights that would make her famous.

Yet all that grit and stick-to-it-iveness, not to mention Coleman's flying skill, couldn't earn her top billing—or let's face it, any billing—in the history books by the time I was an eager middle schooler in the mid-1970s, lapping up all the adventure stories I could. Imagine how powerful it would have been for my peers of color to hear about Bessie Coleman, and how vital for myself, that white kid surrounded by all the toxic racism and racial hierarchies of the time, to revere Queen Bess next to, or better yet instead of, "Lady Lindy," as Earhart was often called.

Both Earhart and Coleman died tragically. Earhart, as we all know, was attempting a round-the-world record, with a final leg entailing a long Pacific crossing of twenty hours and a fuel stop on tiny Howland Island, 2,556 miles from land. Earhart and her navigator never made it to Howland, which was just a two-mile-long speck in a vast heaving ocean, so the odds were always grim. At the date of this writing the plane's fate and any sign of what happened remain unknown. Queen Bess's death was less mysterious but just as dramatic: her mechanic left a wrench in the engine, which slipped midflight, jammed the controls, and sent the Jenny biplane into a dive. Coleman was not flying the plane; she was in the passenger seat scoping out possible landing zones for her latest trick, a jump from its wing with a parachute. The sudden twist threw her (sans parachute) from her seat and she fell to her death. The mechanic, at the yoke, died on impact. White newspapers highlighted the (white, male) mechanic's death, while Black newspapers mourned and lauded Queen Bess; ten thousand people showed up to her funeral.

The takeoff is the embodiment of a decisive moment, the first half of that moment on the earth, the next half airborne. So it is with the Coleman v. Earhart legacies: a small but reverberating fork in the long timeline of history when a white female aviator was elevated and a Black female aviator was left behind. Given the power of a role model, and how much Earhart did to push our notions of what women could and should do, and how deeply the myths of her life and death have permeated our own sense of what it is to be American, I wonder just how radically different our current institutions could have been if it had somehow been Coleman's legacy, not Earhart's, that had prevailed.

Loneliness

My wife is an artist, a very good one, who once explained that while the drawing itself is important, so are the places on the paper where there is no drawing. *White space*, it's called. The white space speaks as much as the pen strokes or the watercolor, she tells me.

A few years later she sits on a beach and sketches the ocean while I surf. Except it isn't the ocean per se. It's me, depicted as a tiny scratch mark dabbed with color, along with seven or so other scratch marks to depict fellow surfers; the rest is white space. Never have I seen anything that so adequately captures how vulnerable and insignificant and eternally hopeful it feels to lurch around on your board, gazing to the horizon and the open sea for something that might propel you shoreward.

Takeoff is that moment you commit to adventure, but also to *loneliness*. There is no other word for it. Being loosed from the earth is both soul-stirring and soul-fraying; you are immediately homesick in a deeply existential way. And why not? All that you are familiar with is dropping away under your feet. You, tiny pilot, are the scratch; the sky, gaping white space.

There is a New Age concept that believes a soul from a living body can soar through the universe, tethered only by a silver cord to its human asleep in the bed, say, or stiff-backed in the lotus position. This "astral projection" allows us to explore nether realms of spirit and time-warp, supposedly. And woe be to you if that silver cord is broken or comes untied—that means death, say the believers.

Where I come from in New England, astral projection would qualify as "nonsense," along with talk therapy, jeans sold with holes in them, and letting dogs sleep in the bed. We chop our own wood, and we drive without panic on ice. We use short, simple sentences, we cut our own bangs. To be a rural New Englander, in other words, is to be eminently practical, with a disdain for the woo-woo.

And yet, flying brings out the mystic in me. I can feel that invisible soul cord unwinding on takeoff, tugging as I gain altitude, tightening way up high. When familiar landscape becomes an unrecognizable higgledy-piggledy of tiny geometries below me and the horizon is suddenly at my feet, I am not just aloft but adrift, like flotsam swept overboard into a heaving sea. It is then that if I am in my paraglider I will glance at the carabiners that attach to the lines that themselves attach to the wing and make sure they are closed; in my trike I will peer at the cables for sudden imperfections. None of this is reasonable but it is somehow reassuring. It is my version of checking the silver cord for its pulse of otherworldly light, its sturdy glinting sheath.

I've flown the gyro as high as 11,000 feet above sea level, but the tops of the Sierra mountains were just a few thousand feet below, so that was not as stomach-churning as when I forced myself to fly 8,000 feet, *one and a half miles*, above ground level to see how it felt. For a pilot encased in a metal fuselage and surrounded by blinking lights, sturdy glass, and a heating system, this altitude is child's play. But perch yourself on an exposed seat in a wisp of an aircraft, and it will take your breath away. There was exhilaration. There was dread. There was bewilderment. And there was this gaping loneliness. And why not. My DNA was once microbe, then pelagic, and now it has spent millions of years developing legs, but never, never did it plan to evolve me into something airborne. And here I am anyway, in defiance of that plodding and determined path. And I am *so small*, dwarfed by white space, far from home. No wonder the pilot Ruth Nichols exclaimed, after her first flight in 1927, "I felt as if my soul was completely freed from my earthly body." (Another pilot of the day, Florence "Pancho" Barnes, who later founded the first stunt pilots' union, had a more colorful description: "Flying," she said, "makes me feel like a sex maniac in a whorehouse with a stack of twenty-dollar bills.")

The skydiver and BASE jumper Felix Baumgartner seems to have had no worries about his own silver cord, which he no doubt stretched to its limit when in 2012 he rode a capsule attached under a balloon to the stratosphere. His plan was a takeoff from the capsule's lip and a free fall from the highest altitude ever recorded. Then he would pull his parachute and land on his own two feet in New Mexico. Remember, jetliners also fly in the stratosphere, but at 30,000 feet. Baumgartner's eventual leap was from almost nineteen miles higher—at 127,852 feet.

It's worth asking why one would attempt such a feat. It doesn't cure hunger or stop wars. Baumgartner was certainly chasing fame, money, adrenaline, and a new metric to prove his mettle: he had already become the first to skydive *across* the English Channel using a special wing, and he held the dubious record for the world's lowest BASE jump. But according to his team of aviators, military personnel, and engineers, this balloon jump was more than just a daredevil stunt. It would advance science. If his fancy pressure suit (in which he was initially very claustrophobic; he overcame this problem with the help of sports psychologists) could withstand the breaking of the sound barrier and speeds of over 800 miles per hour, astronauts could benefit, for example. In fact, aviation has always made progress through record seekers; *The Complete History of Aviation* chronicles the many leaps in technology during the 1920s and '30s that were driven by overland air races, long-distance goals, and speed attempts. The result was deadly planes made available to wreak havoc by World War II, and many advances directly responsible for modern airline travel.

I was one of the eight million people on the ground glued to Baumgartner's live feed on YouTube. We were seeing what he saw from his perch more than twenty-four miles above us: a blazing scrim of atmosphere stopped suddenly by the blackness of space. Below him was our curving planet, its surface just dim shadings, almost blurry. From that height, Earth offered just a shaky promise of topography and firm ground.

The initial moments before his jump were an homage to the checklist—every move he made was dictated by mission control far below: *item 26, move seat to the rear of capsule; item 27, lift legs into the door threshold; item 28, slide the seat forward; item 29, undo seatbelt* . . .

What could be lonelier, I wondered. There was the chummy voice in his ear, sometimes deviating slightly from the script ("attaboy . . . your chute's okay, Felix . . . here we go, item 34"), but otherwise Baumgartner was as far from home and humanity as one person could be (even astronauts do space walks with companions nearby). Of course, there are other ways to feel distant from all that moors you. A friend of mine once said of her failing marriage that the loneliest she ever felt was when her husband was in the same room, and I nodded in agreement.

Baumgarten didn't jettison himself with a dramatic leap. His suit was too bulky for such theatrics. Instead, he *tipped* into oblivion, Humpty Dumpty–style, then dropped so quickly I caught my breath. For a few moments we saw what was happening as if through night vision goggles; the screen showed just a tiny white figure pinned in front of a large gray backdrop. Meanwhile, a voice from mission control counted out increasing speeds against the rasp of Baumgartner's own breathing. Then things went wrong; in the thin air of the stratosphere, Baumgartner began to somersault, which then tightened into a spin. The danger was later graphically and perhaps needlessly explained: If the spin had continued into an irreversible *flat* spin, his own blood would have been pinned up against all his orifices, eventually finding its way out of the only possible opening: his eyeballs. Exsanguination by eyeball, in other words. But Baumgartner managed to right himself as he entered the thicker air of the troposphere, and from there the rest of the jump went smoothly. He broke the record he wanted: highest free fall altitude, previously set in 1960 by his mentor and ground crew member (and the voice in his ear), Joseph Kittinger. During his 4-minute-and-19-second free fall (he missed that record, kept by Kittinger at 4 minutes 36 seconds), Baumgartner also broke the sound barrier—though he says he did not hear a boom—reaching speeds of 843.6 miles per hour, becoming the first person to do so without the help (or protection) of a vehicle.

Baumgartner's record did not stand long. Two years later, the engineer Alan Eustace jumped quietly and without fanfare from 135,890 feet, almost 10,000 feet higher. Why this musical chairs of record breaking? What more has been gained? Eustace has earned wide-eyed acknowledgment that his feat too took courage and engineering (and money), but it is Baumgartner who made that first out-of-the-box effort; everything else after seems a shinier imitation, another layer of thin icing on the proverbial cake.

"Sometimes you have to go really high to understand how small you are," Baumgartner said into his transmitter right before leaping. These words were preplanned; that was lucky, because Baumgartner's goals seemed to change when faced with his view of space. As he explained later to assembled journalists, "Trust me, when you stand up there on top of the world, you become so humble. It's not about breaking records anymore. It's not about getting scientific data. It's all about coming home." Baumgartner, pursuer of limits, challenger of mortal boundaries, was profoundly moved by his imminent takeoff.

Then he gazed down and tipped himself homeward.

13

Fear of Flying

My wife is afraid of flying, and so she often calls from an airport lounge, needing me to explain again why her upcoming flight will not be the one falling out of the sky. She is never asking for facts, just reassurance, but sometimes I can't help myself. "The drive to the airport was statistically more dangerous," I say. "When was the last time a commercial plane crashed, out of thousands of flights daily!" (The real daily number is higher, about forty-five thousand domestic departures a day.) Inevitably the conversation veers to turbulence—"Turbulence is just air," I explain. "We fly through hurricanes, remember."

She calls me again from her middle seat while waiting to depart. *Turbulence is just air*, I repeat. In the background, overhead bells are dinging and flight attendants can be heard telling her to please put away her phone. *Thank you*, she whispers before cutting off the call, the valium in her bloodstream already taking effect.

Why Fly

I have been afraid *while* flying, but I do not have a fear *of* flying, a condition best described as generalized anxiety or aversion to getting on a plane and taking to the air. I understand it, though. A commercial aircraft is a fantastical creature, more so than even my strange-looking gyrocopter. It is an absurdly large metal canister filled with hot dinner rolls, luggage, small liquids, easily removed shoes, here and there an emotional support animal, tiny pretzel packages, and three hundred souls, all suspended at 32.000 feet by . . . what? Nothing visible. No strings above or herculean shoulders below. We peer out the portholes to see only a vernix of clouds, and beneath them (and miles away) our home. No wonder 40 percent of Americans claim to have a fear of flying, and 5 percent refuse to fly at all.

Yet the statistics are clear: commercial flight is very safe. For one thing, the passenger plane is continually inspected like a virus under a microscope, groomed with wrenches and robot arms like a prized thoroughbred, swarmed by eyes at mandated intervals, fed royal jelly. In 2023 there were 37 million commercial aircraft flights globally. Yet there was only one fatal crash—of a turboprop in Nepal that killed 72 people. Compare that to 1.19 million deaths that year by car. In 2024, there were 40.6 million flights; out of that there were seven fatal accidents and 224 deaths. January 2025 brought the high-profile collision of a helicopter and a passenger plane over the Potomac near Ronald Reagan Washington National Airport, but this should fix attention less on the vagaries of flight itself and more on how crowded the skies have become and the pressures on air traffic controllers. You still have only about a 1 in 13.7 *million* chance of dying in a commercial airline accident. Meanwhile, you have a 1 in 93 chance of dying in an automobile. And yet aviophobics abound. They avoid a flight and drive the deadly automobile to their destination instead, nodding in agreement as the facts are thrown at them. *I know, I know*, they say, hands wide. *It's so dumb.* They concede to logic with trilling voices, shrugging shoulders, bobbing heads. But their eyes tell a different story.

For some it's the actual flying. For others it's the tight space, the closing doors, the inability to get off. Still others have real-life experience to point to, often involving turbulence, sometimes lightning. They vow never to get on a plane again. One friend of mine underwent EMDR (eye movement desensitization and reprocessing therapy), which uses bilateral stimulation (moving the eyes is one technique, but also tapping each side of the chest or face, for example) while recalling the past trauma. These stimulations are said to connect the two hemispheres of the brain, grounding the person in the present, therapists say, and blunting the physical sensations attached to the memory. My friend dutifully taps her legs as the doors close, and boards a plane without panic now (though she carries Lorazepam just in case).

Exposure is another fear of flying therapy. Photos of planes are placed at eye level, along with gentle exhortations to breathe. Then videos of airplanes, sounds of airplanes, visits to real airplanes, sitting inside real airplanes. Courses to combat fear of flying take this tack in two-day bites. They explain the physics of flight, they discuss the creaks and groans and roars a plane makes, they offer meditation. Questions are asked and answered by real commercial pilots: No, the wings won't fall off, no, there are no secret codes transmitted from pilot to the crew of catastrophic mechanical failure but kept from passengers. That dreaded turbulence? Captain Steve Allright, who helps run the fear of flying course for British Airways ("Captain Allright knows that his name, too, sounds fictional. It is not," explains a *New York Times* article), assures that even very rough air is "uncomfortable but not dangerous." These courses boast a 98 percent success rate for those who complete it; however, that percentage doesn't tell the whole story: a number of participants walk out of the classroom early or refuse to board for the demonstration flight on the second day. But for those who finish all the steps, the conversion seems thorough. Testimonials afterward show passengers rapturous about the beauty they saw from the window seat, or tearful and elated that they can now join their families on vacation.

Facts, then, can win out. Amanda Ripley wrote about disaster behavior in her book *The Unthinkable*. She says her research, as macabre as it sometimes was, did not make her more fearful. "Having studied dozens of plane crashes," she tells us, "I'm more relaxed when I'm flying . . . the truth, it turns out, is usually better than the nightmare." The nightmare is of precarious physics and weak wing structure, of sudden and catastrophic mechanical failures, of nose-dives into the ground. But the truth? Ripley says that of all serious commercial plane accidents from 1983 to 2000—in other words, those that involve fire, severe injury, and major destruction to the aircraft itself—even then, 56 percent of the people aboard survived.

Researchers have found that our initial reaction to an unfolding disaster is denial. We simply don't believe that something catastrophic is happening. This is because we are steeped in *normalcy bias*, a condition Ripley explains as "a tendency to believe that everything is okay because, well, it almost always has been before." Not helping at all is a human brain that evolved to process reality in patterns so that we register and react quickly. This means we rely on "information from the past to understand what is happening in the present and anticipate the future." This pattern making from familiarity is foundational; researchers have discovered that brains can go into neural overload when confronted with the sheer strangeness of a disaster that doesn't follow any previous template. Unable to process what is happening, people report losing their sight or their hearing. Others find themselves unable to move. Flight attendants were once trained to give instructions in quiet voices so as not to elicit panic; now they are told to shout in terse and demanding tones to break through passengers' neural confusion during an emergency.

The safety briefing at the beginning of each flight is usually dismissed as a boring pantomime, a chance to instead rummage into our phones or our bags or our movies on our tablets. But an analysis of accidents by the NTSB finds that those who watched that briefing, even if they had seen it many times before, *had a higher chance of escaping injury or death.* These dutiful passengers were unwittingly taking advantage of our neural need for previous patterns; as the real emergency unfolded the brain so recently steeped in inflatable slide instruction and floor lighting explication better grasped what was happening.

I venture to guess that aviophobes might react better in a disaster than the nonphobic Pollyannas around them. These fear-of-flying folks have circumvented the denial phase that overwhelms because, after all, they have been expecting this cataclysm. So, while I will still assure that flying is safe, let's anticipate disaster anyway. Read the laminated safety instructions, count the number of seats forward and aft to the exits, put down phones/tablets/books and watch as flight attendants mime oxygen flow, buckle belts, reach for imaginary flotation cushions. Engage your brain in disaster patterns, why not?

"Down!" my wife texts upon landing. "THANK YOU."

PART 5

FLIGHT (OUTBOUND)

Everyone has oceans to fly, if they have the heart to do it. Is it reckless? Maybe. But what do dreams know of boundaries?

AMELIA EARHART

14

The View

The American astronaut Leland Melvin remembers eating a meal with his colleagues while in orbit on the International Space Station, everyone pointing out their home country as it spun by in a tapestry of night, day, green, brown, blue. "And that's when this shift happened . . . the human piece of us sharing and breaking bread and seeing the planet in that way. Our respective homes, up in space." Adds the Canadian fighter pilot and engineer Chris Hadfield, who spent 166 days circling Earth, "I took a picture, actually, of Karachi, Pakistan, and I read what I wrote about it the next day, which was: 'There are 6 million of us living in Pakistan.' And I realized that that part of the world had become *us* for me."

So powerful was this view from above that one veteran made a habit of leading new astronauts to the observation cupola atop the International Space Station with their eyes closed for maximum effect. When their eyes opened and they gazed upon the earth below, "every single crew member I brought in there for that exposure, cried."

This exposure is called the *overview effect*, a swell of specific emotions and perspectives triggered by seeing our planet in space, far away. *Connected, connected, everything is connected*, the astronauts say over and over when explaining that utter astonishment at the blue marble of their home hung against the infinite, the curious bloom inside them. You don't see the nation-state boundaries, they point out, the artificially drawn lines between countries and towns. Instead, it is interplay and flow on display in shifting, seeping, melting colors and shapes. In her prizewinning novel *Orbital*, Samantha Harvey writes of her own imaginary astronauts, "Everything that speaks of being in space—which is everything—ambushes them with happiness, and it isn't so much that they don't want to go home but that home is an idea that has imploded—grown so big, so distended and full, that it's caved in on itself."

The real astronaut Mae Jemison agrees with this expanding aperture concept. She writes that her reaction "wasn't a connection back down to Earth. It was a connection to the rest of the universe." She says that imagining herself a citizen on a star millions of miles from Earth did not seem strange or scary: "For me it was about 'outward' versus 'inward.'"

Another significant theme for those who experience the overview effect: a sudden visceral understanding of fragility, and a newfound wash of concern for rivers and oceans and air. Indeed, the man who coined and first studied the overview effect, the author Frank White, linked it not just to seeing Earth but also to gazing at the blue layer of atmosphere that is our tenuous protection against black space. Muses an International Space

Station crew member in the documentary film *Overview*, "The only border that matters is that thin blue line."

White first imagined the overview effect while pondering the future space colonist who would peer at her planet from a distant one. Lacking those colonists at the time, he interviewed astronauts in orbit. It wasn't exactly deep space and a floating planet unimaginably far away, but it was good enough (technically, space begins 62 miles, 100 kilometers, up, delineated by an imaginary boundary called the Kármán line). Since then, other scientists have studied the overview effect, defining it as the "overwhelming emotion and feelings of identification with humankind and the planet as a whole" when Earth is viewed from space. They note that those who experience the overview effect (not all astronauts do) report more compassion and a profound shift in identity. They see themselves suddenly as part of a larger whole. They feel small but not insignificant.

"We stand there gaping," Harvey writes. "And in time we come to see that not only are we on the sidelines of the universe, but that it is a universe of sidelines, that there is no center, just a giddy mass of waltzing things, and that perhaps the entirety of our understanding consists of an elaborate and ever-evolving knowledge of our own extraneousness, a bashing away of mankind's ego by the instruments of scientific enquiry until it is, that ego, a shattered edifice that lets light through."

Yet most of us will never get to space. Does this mean that the overview effect is beyond our grasp? How much altitude must one really gain to trigger this cascade, these astonished realizations, these emotions and reassessments? White himself first wondered about the overview effect while peering at the landscape below from an ordinary airplane in the early 1970s. So perhaps we can access something of this magic and connection while in everyday lower-level flight.

I had long thought that my dominant sensation when I flew was adrenaline. I was once genuinely thrilled to be head-butted by inversion boundaries, jabbed by turbulence, and left-hooked by rising thermals. This chaos was common for the large, light, experimental wings I flew, and so I chalked it up to proof of adventure, proof of flying. But as I got older I realized that I was no longer eager for or even indifferent to getting thrown about. I began to avoid the tightened jaw and sweat down the neck. Instead, I exulted over the blue-yellow tint of a winter day. I marveled at the tule elk, looking like strewn paperclips accidentally dropped on a carpet of green. I went into boring detail about a coyote who stopped midstride, head cocked to the chuckling, whining, rumbling sound above, calculating whether it was a threat and concluding that it was not. My interests were the wild mane of trees that passed under my feet, the ropy freeways, the prissy squares of suburban houses laid out on a grid. This being California, those houses are soon destroyed by wildfire, leaving only lonely cul-de-sacs and bereft chimneys. It would take months, even years, before the white dots of cement trucks would appear and the yellow of plywood walls would shine in the sun, but nearby a meadow quickly came back to iridescent green life. Stupefied by its resilience, I would circle, stare, circle, stare, feel my own blooming heart. I lacked words. I was all exhale. This my own overview effect, more mundanely explained as *being in awe*.

As Annie Murphy Paul states in her book *The Extended Mind*, awe can be induced by anything that feels otherworldly, vast, powerful—"the gaping hugeness of the Grand Canyon or the crashing grandeur of Niagara Falls," for instance. Awe is a reaction of wonder, veneration, perhaps dread, to a grand mystery; it is the overview effect as felt in low Earth orbit.

In the past decade, the concept of awe has broken into the mainstream, with whole books that explain what triggers it, how to access it, and why it's good for us. Notably, researchers find that awe scrambles old neural patterns, thus overturning assumptions and defying preconceived notions. For this reason, it makes us more open-minded and more curious and tilts us into a "radically new perspective," says Murphy Paul, one that underscores our proportional significance, or lack of it, in a wider universe. Surprisingly, this perspective results not in alienation and nihilism, but in that feeling of deep connection that the astronauts talk about; we are not the center of things but part of a larger whole.

Awe can be triggered by a sublime ballet jump or a hike among wildflowers, yes, but a change in vantage point—suddenly feeling physically tiny in the face of a natural wonder, or, say, from above, in the air—can be especially awe-inducing. In his memoir about regularly flying the mail across treacherous routes like the Andes and the Sahara, Antoine de Saint-Exupéry writes, "But by the grace of the airplane [I] have been made to ponder with even more bewilderment the fact that this earth that is our home is yet in truth a wandering star." With this sentence he expresses his own awe, his own place in a larger schema, his sudden sense that he is piloting through, not just a sky, but a universe. He is experiencing the overview effect.

We have a chance, then, to experience this type of awe every time we board a commercial flight. But most of us at window seats don't look out with much more than mild curiosity. We don't let ourselves be awed, or perhaps awe is tamped down by the way that a modern plane forces its heavy, cramped, noisy insides on us. Or maybe we are just inured to wonder; we've seen the views on television and on computer screens, so what's the big deal? Yet if we let ourselves look with full attention, allow awe to blow our neural system a little bit, we realize as White did that "the earth is one system, that we are all part of that system, and that there is a certain unity and coherence to it all."

And so I fly just after dawn along my favorite beach, which will go unnamed, where morning light drops tinsel on the ocean, elephant seals sleep in commas on the sand, and a stork rises from the nearby marsh like a fleeting thought; it is not uncommon for me to be rocked by a sudden hurtling of my heart, and to cry.

Low and Slow

Georgia O'Keeffe, the American modernist painter, was transformed by the bird's-eye view. Most known for her close-ups of flowers, and her semiabstract landscapes, she began to regularly travel by airplane in the late fifties. She had always been intrigued by the sky from the ground; now she was astounded by this higher perspective. And so began her famous cloudscape series.

O'Keeffe's first flight-inspired painting featured a curving green island seen below small penguin-shaped clouds. Her initial intention appears to have been to emphasize the land; a sketch she made from the plane is mostly of the island itself. But the finished piece instead highlights the clouds, says the educator and artist Grace Almanza in a lecture at the Georgia O'Keeffe Museum, and the island, though center, seems to be dissolving.

Over the next four paintings the landscape disappears completely, and O'Keeffe perfects her depiction of clouds, transforming them from loosely edged and penguiny to precisely outlined "little oval white clouds," as she described them. Eventually O'Keeffe paints her largest piece ever, an 8-foot-tall by 24-foot-long cloudscape over which flows an orange-blue-yellow sky. "Such a size is of course ridiculous," O'Keeffe said of the work when it went on display, but for a pilot like me such a size seems essential. How else to capture the exploding light, the very audacity of the infinite? O'Keeffe never painted on that large a canvas again, but flying in planes continued to intrigue and inspire her; she completed eleven cloudscapes in all.

The journalist and pilot William Langewiesche is also a fan of the bird's-eye view, but he doesn't want it to skid by underneath at a great speed or height. Though he writes often of commercial jets, sturdy cargo planes, and nimble Cessnas, he is most enchanted by an unlikely and often unloved craft: the simple and lowly paraglider. In his book *Aloft*, he lauds the paraglider wing's slow amble across the sky, its unobstructed views, the steady onrush of wind that can seem like silence, and he wants everyone—pilot and non-pilot alike—to grab a helmet, belt in, run down a hill, and launch. This recommendation is only half facetious; mostly it is wistful, with the air of someone who knows the suggestion is a little over-the-top and that he is speaking to a world that has bundled risk in bubble wrap and set it carefully aside.

Langewiesche does acknowledge that the paraglider is dangerous. It is, after all, just a wing-shaped canopy attached by thin nylon lines to a harness in which a human can sit. This inherently flimsy design makes it slow to react and prey to strong winds. Yet the very lumbering and unpredictable quality of this unlikely kite, Langewiesche argues, is what allows a human to see the world from the perfect vantage and speed. "Indulge in the risk," he coaxes, because it is worth it. Low, but not too low, and slow; this allows for the most intimate connection to our home. "Imagine," he muses, "the arrival of an entire generation in which people truly had learned to see their world from above." Though he never uses the term, what could this be but Langewiesche urging that we expose ourselves to our own overview effect?

In the 1980s I unwittingly took Langewiesche's advice. I believed in seeing the world from above but had tired of Cessnas, which were expensive to fly and felt like being encased in a soup can. I began to pilot paragliders. The sport was new: the wing still in its rudimentary phases of design, and the instructors yahoos learning the ins and outs themselves. These factors meant that paraglider flight was much more dangerous than I ever let on to friends and family.

Many maneuvers were a mystery at the time, constantly being tested. For one, there were questions about spiral dives, a skill used to lose altitude, or simply to experience the sudden squeeze of G-forces for kicks. A spiral dive resembles a steep, continuous 360-degree turn but it differs in that your wing is banked so sharply that you seem to fall as well as spin. This was a common maneuver for us, but soon there was mounting suspicion that something was amiss. It seemed that periodically and for unknown reasons the wing would refuse to unlock from its whirling descent; sadly, the main witness was often dead, so it was hard to confirm the issue. Soon pilots were also attempting to do what now seems to be easy—a 360-degree loop. I knew a pilot who fell back into his canopy as he reached the nadir, became hopelessly entwined, plummeted to the ground, and died. These sorts of flaws and pushings of possibilities abounded until enough accidents gave rise to newer, safer designs (whereupon new boundaries were then pushed, of course).

Partial wing collapses were common, but also highly feared. A wing collapse is just what it sounds like: a nerve-jangling unshaping of part of the flying wing into a flapping piece of cloth. If the collapses were small enough, they could be reinflated. Sometimes if you didn't catch it quickly the wing could begin to spin, or drop, the material tangled irretrievably in the lines that attached it to the harness.

There were times, however, when circumstances required that you *initiate* a wing collapse. Not just a partial one—a total one. This meant mutating the whole wing into an ineffectual rag on purpose. These total wing collapses, also known as stalls, were executed to get out of an extreme wind event, and indeed I once faced this very predicament, along with this barbarous choice.

The half-baked plan that preceded this folly involved a new type of flying for me, called *thermal flying*. This is what those glider pilots in the 1930s sought to understand when they visited South America. Thermal flying is a way of finding lift by locating and then rising upward in a column of hot air known as a thermal. This is very different from the "soaring" that I had learned, in which I relied on the topography of California cliffs for buoyancy—specifically, wind coming in off the sea that deflected upward and formed a fairly reliable "band" of upward push. The length of the lift band, as we called it, was roughly the length of the cliff, the width of it varied but was easily, and without much ado, marked out after studying the topography or simply flying it at a safe altitude and noting when the paraglider would begin to descend.

On this day, however, I found myself in Brazil launching from a volcano. No cliffs were in sight, but 3,000 feet below me the vast, flat, dark plain broiled in the midday sun and shot robust columns of hot air skyward. These thermals were marked by circling birds, if we were lucky, but also by fluffy white clouds. All around the sky I could see these bulging muscles of shifting cumulus marking where the hotter air of a rising thermal met a colder layer. Here it cooled, condensed, and stopped rising.

It would be my very first day of thermal flying, and I was eager but nervous. I launched and made my way toward circling birds. After a few clumsy attempts at gaining altitude, I skirted away to look for something else. I wasn't worried, the sky was full of possibility, and soon enough I found myself ascending. So excited was I to find a thermal, and also so new to this type of flying, I didn't fully understand that I was rising too fast. Nor did I inspect closely the cloud congealing above me. Turns out it was no fluffy, genial cumulus cloud, but a heaving, building cumulo*nimbus* cloud. It had a gray underside and, unbeknownst to me, an expanding topside.

Cumulonimbus: also known as a freaking-scary-towering-*storm*-cloud.

I was being cloud-sucked.

In these cases, the thermal does not stop at the bottom of the cloud. It rushes into it and keeps rising, so you are borne upward into complete and terrifying darkness, not to mention lightning, ice, wind, and hail.

I knew about the terror of cloud-suck from the saga of two professional paraglider pilots who had experienced it during a competition. Only one lived to tell the tale. She was pulled upward to *32,000 feet* (this was recorded by her instruments and tracked by her ground team) and along the way lost consciousness. Miraculously, the thundercloud coughed her out with her paraglider still intact, or maybe not intact and she threw her reserve, I cannot remember. Either way, she gained consciousness after dropping tens of thousands of feet, and maneuvered herself to the ground. Her compatriot suffered a more typical fate: buffeted by the stormy interior, lacking oxygen, his clothes torn off and his paraglider ripped to shreds, he fell to his death.

But none of this was yet on my mind as I hurtled upward. Instead, I was gleeful. I was triumphant, self-congratulatory, almost chuckling at how quickly I had picked up what was supposedly so difficult. Look at me! In a thermal! Like a bird! I leveled my wing as the cloud base approached, knowing that the rising air was cooling, and would slow my ascent, and, after all, I was such a natural, yes, and I could already see my balletic traverse to the next invisible elevator. But my ascent did not slow. It quickened. I must have been puzzled, but my beginner brain was lagging behind the facts, and it was only as the mist encircled me that I realized: cloud suck.

I had only milliseconds to successfully escape. The protocol, I knew, was to initiate the complete wing collapse/stall. Let it be said, however, that to collapse a wing in order to drop like a stone in the middle of the sky is still against one's better instincts no matter how much your brain tells you it is the right course of action. This maneuver would entail pulling hard on both of my toggles and pressing my fists against my thighs, holding them there until the wing acquiesced and dropped into a tight ball behind me. What was once an airfoil would now be reshaped into something closer to sheets tossed on the floor after you pull them from a bed. No longer a wing but a buffeting piece of colored cloth. Then the plan would be to willingly plummet for hundreds of feet until clear of the danger, whereupon I would bring my arms back up and do what it took to reinflate the wing to its natural shape. Two events could unfold at this point. First, the shock of the reinflation might be so abrupt that I would swing wildly. This could happen with such force as to deflate the wing again—or, it was said, you could fall back into your wing, whereupon it would wrap around you like a burial shroud, and become one. The second thing that might happen is that the stalled wing would become tangled in its lines and never reinflate. Here I would deploy my reserve chute, pull in the traitorous wing, and hope the two didn't entwine irretrievably in the process. I was no novice: I had executed this maneuver over a lake in a safety clinic and had watched others do the same. In the end we'd all landed just fine, but it had been heart-stopping. This was why, despite the horrible danger I knew I faced within the storm cloud, my instincts cowered before the shrine of the dreaded stall.

In a flash of dubious genius, I decided on a less extreme emergency maneuver, reasoning that I could fall back (so to speak) on the stall if nothing else worked. First: "big ears," in which you pull the tips of the wing inward to make the shape smaller, causing you to drop. I pulled the biggest big ears I had ever used, halving my wing area. Still I kept rising, faster now, and the world whited out completely. Swiftly I executed that aforementioned spiral dive, *while still in big ears*. This time it worked: the white began to mist and suddenly I could see the ground again. I had broken free of the thundercloud's grip.

Later I went over this terrifying situation with a paragliding instructor; the stall, he explained, would have been the best choice, as fearsome and uncertain as it was at that time. Spiral dives and big ears were not meant to be combined, he told me, as that put too much strain on the wing. The upshot was that I had been lucky. The whole kit and caboodle could have ripped apart at the seams, dashing me onto the Brazilian plain.

Why Fly

So why did I continue flying paragliders, given the perils? Langewiesche would understand. Of all the aircraft I've piloted, the paraglider wing offers the purest form of flight: quick to foot-launch, quiet except for the low whistle of air passing over fabric, slow enough to see all that you want to see as you soar by. It is birdlike flying—in fact, a friend of mine swore one day that a hawk landed on his wing as he flew, which I did not witness, and whether it's true or not, it speaks to the fanciful kinship we felt with our avian companions. We were followed by seagulls and chased by ground birds protecting their nests and dived upon by hawks, all of which led us to believe, incorrectly, that we were part of their world and not crass and clumsy interlopers.

Still, forgoing engines and metal frames meant the paraglider had narrow wind parameters, and so we spent many afternoons speed-dialing the phone number for the automated wind sensors and bemoaning the conditions from home, or worse, hanging around at launch gazing mournfully at the sky, an exercise that we called *parawaiting*. Finally, after a decade and a half of paragliding, I decided to switch back to powered craft.

Years later I returned to the sport one more time, strapping myself to the chest of a champion paraglider named Dave Turner. During the flight I asked him to execute the most extreme maneuver he knew. I cannot tell you exactly what it entailed, except that the world flew by me at all angles, seemingly at once. There was no way that the wings I had once flown could have performed this maneuver (really a series of maneuvers) without fatally collapsing or otherwise losing control. It was then that I realized just how rudimentary my own equipment had been, and how far its flying design had come. My own beloved intermediate wing had been considered the minivan of canopies when I was flying it, stable and reliable, but when I passed it on to a friend a few years after I left the sport, his instructor took one look at it and pronounced it "a death trap." This underscores how far and fast a new sport progresses, and that if you catch it near its inception you will unwittingly be part of a grand experiment with equipment that goes from incredibly sketchy to sort of okay to eventually reliable.

. . .

It was with a dose of luck, then, that the first airplane fatality happened a good five years after the Wrights' Flyer officially achieved controlled flight. In 1908, the Flyer augered into the ground with Orville at the helm; Orville escaped death, his passenger did not. Brother Wilbur waxed philosophical, saying, "If you are looking for perfect safety, you will do well to sit on a fence and watch birds, but if you really wish to learn you must mount a machine and become acquainted with its tricks by actual trial." He and other pioneers of flight knew: good training keeps you safe, but if you're doing that training in the nascent stages of that endeavor, with so many unknowns, there are variables that can overwhelm. Your luck runs out. But often it holds—your wing stays intact, you land safely, you slow your catapulting heart and declare yourself wiser. And through it all you find the wonder Langewiesche promises, staying low and slow, looking down from above, wanting more.

16

Birds

That slender mechanism, the wing. Watching it so closely for so long, we humans finally designed a mostly ugly approximation. On birds, meanwhile, it remains a marvel, sometimes a jagged scimitar slicing air, other times buffing the sky. It angles, flaps, changes shape. So how does it actually work, this multitasking lever?

Turns out that most of the wing from the shoulder outward, known as the *arm-wing*, functions as a typical airfoil—air goes over and under, creating lift. But as you reach the tips (the *hand-wing*), things start to work differently. The hand-wing articulates in ways that create low-pressure vortices, or swirling "tornadoes" as scientists describe them, to keep the bird flying. These vortices allow for quick and tight direction changes. It finally explains how birds can touch down so precisely on a tree branch.

The physics tells us that a slowing airspeed brings a corresponding loss of lift; if it was just the arm-wing in play, a landing bird would need to approach gradually, lose airspeed incrementally, and then at the right altitude—say, a few centimeters from the intended spot—and at such slight lift and low forward speed that, with a flick that upturns the wing only slightly (which we call the *flare*), her bird legs now safely reach for earth and take over. This is how most human-made aircraft land, and this is what a runway allows for but a foliage-covered twig does not. Vortices, on the other hand, create great lift and great drag, allowing birds to zig and zag past leaf and trunk. They slow suddenly (drag) yet remain aloft (lift), then stick the branch landing with the decisiveness of a Simone Biles finish. These vortices mean that birds avoid the dreaded stall on approach; the airflow is insufficient to keep them flying, but wingtip tornadoes take over instead.

Some insist that bees break all the rules of flight, given their heavy, rounded bodies and their tiny wings. So say the internet and a few documentaries, usually made by people who want to prove the existence of a God who does what He pleases just to confound and amaze us. Look! A creature that doesn't obey science! Yet the truth is more straightforward: bees generate only vortices to fly, eschewing any arm-wing lift.

Consider too the vortex magic of the small, darting swift, which learns to fly at one month old and doesn't look back, staying aloft for two to three years. These "flickering silhouettes at 30, 40, 50 miles an hour, a shoal of birds," as the naturalist Helen Macdonald describes them, not only mate midflight but also sleep while airborne. They do this by shutting off half of their brain—this is called *unihemispheric slow wave flight*—while the other half stays awake to monitor altitude and potential threats.

Macdonald writes of the way the swifts' calls, so high in the air, seem "less like sound and more like suspicions of glass and dust," and fall silent as the birds ascend in what scientists call a *vesper flight.* "Vesper" means "evening" in Latin; vespers are prayers murmured at dusk. High up, this prayer of swifts (usually called a scream of swifts, but this feels inapt) drift with half their brain asleep, the other half vigilant. In fact, Macdonald suggests that they might fully slumber, and cites a report from a World War II fighter pilot who descended from 10,000 feet with his engine off into "a strange flight of birds, which seemed to be motionless, or at least showed no noticeable reaction." Macdonald writes of the incident: "The remote air, the coldness, the stillness, and the high birds over white clouds suspended in sleep. It's an image that drifts in and out of my dreams."

Vesper flights ascend not just at nautical dusk, but at nautical dawn as well—remember, both are called *nautical twilight*, that time twice a day when the sky is light enough to see the dim outline of the horizon and some of the brighter stars, thus enabling navigation at sea. It is thought that this is the way swifts take stock of incoming weather and realign with the navigational pull of magnetic north, looking to and fro just above the convective boundary layer, where heaving air currents from the earth are no longer a factor and are now replaced by a steady wind. From this vantage point the birds assess where they are and what lies ahead, and Macdonald finds in this a worthy lesson. Swifts aren't always at these "dizzying heights; most of the time they live in thick and complicated air." But to solve problems, the swifts "must go higher to survey the wider scene," Macdonald notes, "and there communicate with others about the larger forces impinging on their realm."

And what can we learn of *murmurations*, those Etch-a-Sketch riots across the sky? The painters are starlings, brought to the United States at the end of the nineteenth century by an amateur ornithologist (some fancifully claim he wanted all the birds mentioned in Shakespeare let loose in Central Park). The first one hundred became over time millions, spread around the country. Quickly they were considered pests but also flying phenomena. The writer Annie Dillard describes watching as the skies darkened and the birds "strayed toward me, transparent and whirling. They seemed to unravel as they flew, lengthening in curves, like a loosened skein." She stands for half an hour, enveloped by "the sound of beaten air, like a million shook rugs, a muffled whuff. Into the woods they sifted without shifting a twig, right through the crowns of the trees, intricate and rushing like wind."

Hand-wings at play for sure, but more too. For so long we didn't understand how starlings could fly in unison as they do, sometimes up to half a million birds at a time. It took a computer simulation to realize: there is no one leader in a murmuration. Every starling, flying as fast as 90 miles per hour, follows seven or so nearby companions. Each sticks to three rules: move toward, turn with, give room. The result is a twisting, churning, shading, cascading, caterwauling, blurring helix. It is chaos and order at once.

The starlings' skill at complex movement in the air underscores humankind's failure at it on the ground, the way crowds stampede regularly, disastrously, killing hundreds, even thousands of us at a time. The crush at Walmart during a 2008 Black Friday sale, for instance, or in the pedestrian tunnel approaching Mecca in 1990. Some of our ineptitude is due to simple physics. According to researcher G. Keith Still, humans need about one square yard to stay upright and moving. In a large crowd, a sudden change to that means the space around us tightens and people become off-balance. Inevitably someone falls and the result is people pushing to help them up, which further aggravates movement and causes a crush. Mostly, though, we lack the temperament of the starling. We need to know what the holdup is, say, when the doors to the concert hall/department store/soccer stadium don't open in time, or a crowded street funnels into a narrow alley. We crane our necks to see, push forward for information. Are birds so impatient or needy? Seems not. They simply follow the seven others. "The difference is that we are selfish individuals," the behavioral scientist Iain Couzin tells John Seabrook, who writes of this inherent human ineptitude at swarm intelligence in his *New Yorker* article examining stampedes and crushes. "We want to reduce our travel time, even when it is at the expense of others . . . In this respect, we are at our most primitive in crowds. We have never evolved a collective intelligence to function in large crowds." Starlings—these flying rhizomes, these mosh pit experts—offer us both sad rebuke and hope.

Find a feather on the ground, run a finger along its gossamer edges. Wonder at its rigid hollow stem, guess at the bird from whom it fell. Feathers are for communication and warmth, but also key to flight, of use in glide, but also flap. This movement, generating both thrust and lift on, say, a windless day, is made particularly efficient by the way a bird wing can bend and resist to differing degrees. Feathers twist and separate on the upstroke to limit drag, then flow back into a solid surface on the downstroke, maximizing lift. The flap is Newton's Third Law of Motion made manifest, equal and opposite actions and reactions in an up/down embroidery stitching the sky.

Look now at the mighty albatross, she who eschews the flap, who is almost all arm-wing (sometimes reaching a total span of over eleven feet) and who is purported to glide nonstop up to five hundred miles in a day. To accomplish this seemingly impossible feat, she deftly employs a flying strategy that involves

Why Fly

dipping up and down, a flight move that a trike pilot friend of mine used often and called "dolphining" but should be renamed "albatrossing." (This is not to be confused with the common overcorrections of a novice pilot that results in increasingly uncontrollable "porpoising.") To this undulation the albatross adds well-timed direction changes, all to minimize wing movement and optimize wind energy and momentum. There is also a unique shoulder locking mechanism that allows the huge wing to stay extended without fatigue, the avian equivalent of tightening the string on a camping tent to keep it from sagging in the wind.

Sailors did not know of the albatross's mighty flying skill, so no wonder it was considered bad luck when an albatross hit the mast of a ship; why else would a huge bird appear suddenly in the middle of the vast ocean unless it was sent by the gods as portent of a storm or malfeasance? Nor did these seamen know that albatrosses sleep on the wing, because they too rest half their brain at a time. Always partially awake, they are aided by mechanisms in their nostrils that calculate air pressure, similar to my aircraft's Pitot tube, making even the dozing bird alert to changes in altitude. This is how the albatross maintains straight and level flight while in (half) slumber, enough to keep from crashing into the ocean but not enough to see and avoid the absurdity that is one lone treelike object sticking up from said waters.

The albatross's deft soar has been named *dynamic glide* by scientists eager to apply it to our own aircraft innovations. In fact, we keep a keen eye on what many birds do, hoping to copy what has already been perfected by millions of years of evolution. (We also study snakes, as some jump from high branches, then flatten and "swim" their body in a way that allows them to glide to another tree up to 60 feet away. This aerial undulation is of great interest for the robotic simulators we are designing to at once efficiently fly, swim, and make their way through sand.) Consider too peregrine falcons, who descend so fast on their prey (250 miles per hour!) that they need a baffle in their nose to diffuse the onrush of air and escape lung annihilation; this is an innovation we appropriated for jet engines.

Birds use their bodies in different ways: When gannets dive seaward they do so with wings angled like an F-14, then retract them tight to their bodies just before they strike the water, turning into missiles instead. Seabirds seem to feint in midair, cartwheeling back to execute their dive, but this is to just protect their trachea from the cudgel that is the ocean met at high speed. Pelicans routinely drop in a ribbon toward an incoming ocean swell and then skim along the underside of the wave, their wingtips just micromillimeters from the shifting water. This technique remained mysterious to scientists, much as many components of waves themselves were mysterious (take the sudden hundred-foot rogue wave in the middle of a quiet ocean, long considered a myth, recently proven to be real); now it's clear that the pelicans use the compressed air bubble created by the arcing wave to do what is called *wave slope soaring*. We pilots experience something similar when our own wings push air against the earth, called "ground effect," but not with such dexterity—rarely do birds skew sideways as we do on takeoff, rarely do they bounce as we do on landing. Only once did I see it: a pigeon biffed his return to a sidewalk with a stumble and a wild wing swing to recover, and I remember laughing in delight. I wasn't gloating, nor did I wish him ill (he wasn't hurt, except perhaps for his bird pride)—it's just that I was relieved to see that flight had its less elegant days for everyone.

A moment now for the arctic terns, who fly halfway around the world to Antarctica to spend the winter, then return to the Arctic in the spring, embedding stopovers during which they feed and rest for the next leg. The trip is not one straight line, but meanders to take advantage of winds, so that a tern may rack up as much as fifty thousand miles in a year. Other bird migrations (20 percent of all birds migrate) don't have stopovers at all—the longest being that of the bar-tailed godwit, which flies more than seven thousand miles without landing.

Pigeons are described as "flying rats," but why? Iridescent breasts, sharp cornering flight, an ability to adapt to whatever is thrown their way—what's not to admire? They ricochet through narrow alleys like echoes, then roost in long gossiping rows, a collegial book club also catching up on the friend-group news. The dangers of urban life are many for pigeons—it is common to see their toes tangled with plastic trash, string, and the worst culprit, human hair. I often approach making sympathetic pigeon sounds with the vague intention of first aid, but immediately each juts out her purple-green breast, takes a step or two on her knotted feet, and, with a noisy flap, flies expertly out of reach. It is worth noting that for all the bells and whistles, manned aircraft cannot yet fly like that—with such speedy hops, and lightning-quick feints, and short parabolas of flight (helicopter and paraglider flight approximates these maneuvers, perhaps, but not with the speed).

So what is it with the slurs, the name calling? We once highly valued the pigeon, known then as the rock dove. We stole them from their cliffs five thousand years ago and used them for food and pets and, most important, to send messages back and forth to lords of distant realms, or perhaps to lovers far away. Pigeons were also lifelines during war; there are numerous examples of humans saved because crucial pigeon-carried messages got through from the perilous front. These birds had names like Commando, Spike, Paddy, and Cher Ami, and they were subjected to all sorts of indignities on our behalf: in World War I, say, they were taken aloft in planes with messages attached to their legs and thrown from the cockpit to hasten their flight; others carried heavy cameras for "aerial reconnaissance." Meanwhile they were also mercilessly shot at and killed or maimed; those that lived might win useless human medals to commemorate their heroics.

When the telegraph line came into being, then the radio, the satellite, the smart phone, the drone, we promptly forgot the pigeons' once sleek trajectories in the service of logistics, love, and battle. We discarded them, then kvetched as they continued to settle in our cities, making use of our own cliff-like structures—the overpass or the skyscraper—and settled for our detritus too. Turns out that pigeons themselves carry no more diseases for you than your cat or dog, probably fewer, and certainly fewer than your child or workmate or average city bus. They groom incessantly. It is humans who leave filth (and hair!) on city streets. If it's edible, sure, a pigeon might be seen making the most of it. They routinely feast on, say, a discarded burrito in the middle of a busy thoroughfare, flap-jumping away right before the oncoming car passes over them only to return and go at it again; if this was a human, they'd be considered resourceful and skilled and their tech company immediately funded. Next time you see a pigeon, remember that we put them here, bred them for human contact, and then abandoned them. And yet they persist, and more than that, they don't seem to harbor a similar ill will, and might even forgive us.

Since we are talking city birds, say hello to the parrots seen partying all over San Francisco. Just this morning I pointed out a slew of cherry-headed conures to a woman walking her dog. This unlikely sight, tropical birds bouncing around a native California tree arguing in the cold and fog of this fair city, made both of us gape, and she repeatedly lowered her sunglasses as if to double-check that the shimmering colors weren't a hallucination. Longtime San Francisco residents know their story: these are the descendants of parrots brought here by the exotic pet trade in the 1980s and early 1990s and sold to humans who think a caged bird will be a submissive bird. Instead, many species of parrot are demanding, and they communicate with screeches that sound very much like a subway train slowing into a station; fed-up owners, the theory goes, shooed them out the apartment window when they'd had enough. I love the parrots here, symbols of freedom, and of life uncaged, and of adaptation, not to mention a healthy fuck-you to humans. They are a reminder that not everything can be fully subjugated. Daily they carouse overhead, exclaiming, cackling, rejoicing in unlovely squawks, winking green and red across the sky.

One final shout-out for an unusual flying inspiration: fish. While the 1940s actress Hedy Lamarr was most famous for her films and her legendary beauty, she has recently been recognized for her many patents and inventions, including "frequency hopping," which was of vital importance during World War II and became "Secret Communication System," U.S. Patent 2,292,387. Less well known is the innovative wing shape she conceived for the aviation mogul Howard Hughes. "I thought [his] airplane wings were too slow. I decided that was not right. They shouldn't be square, the wings. So, I bought a book of fish. And I bought a book of birds, and then I used the fastest bird and connected it with the fastest fish. And I drew it together and I showed it to Howard Hughes. And he said, you're a genius."

Maps

The sky looks wide and open, but for pilots it teems with boundaries and corresponding regulations. Less crowded airspace engenders fewer rules; as you get closer to busier airports, and then very busy airports, the regulations ramp up. The point is simple: to keep aircraft from crashing into each other. This is why rules while in the air speak mostly to visibility parameters and communication. These are the main inflection points, the causes of accidents with other aircraft or with the ground.

You can fly using only instruments to guide you or you can fly using your own eyes outside the cockpit. I fly under the latter, called, fittingly, *visual flight rules*, or VFR in shortspeak. This means I can fly only when I can see for a certain number of miles, and when I can maintain prescribed distances from cloud cover. My rudimentary craft also bristles with an array of communication equipment like radios, transponders, and

ADS-B, all of which allow me to enter busy areas and be tracked by other planes and by air traffic controllers.

Once I am airborne, there are no street signs, no speed limits posted, no Beware of Dog placards, no white picket fence to delineate someone else's property. So how can I know when the airspace and its corollary rules change? For this I consult a large laminated aeronautical chart (also known as a *VFR sectional*), which is tied to my leg so the wind can't snatch it away. Here I find the regulations for my current part of the sky, and what lies ahead.

Looking at a sectional is much like squinting at a treasure map drawn by a thousand schoolchildren hopped up on sugary cereal, so dense is it with color and line, stick symbol, and grawlix. Even a pilot steeped in its secret codes and markings can be easily overwhelmed. These days technology allows us to view our maps on computer tablets (similarly secured to a thigh when in an open cockpit), so visual clutter is eliminated by clearing certain layers. But no matter how the VFR sectional is displayed, it maintains the gravitas and portent of a religious text. It codifies chaos and offers redemption, and pilots are reverential in its presence.

So how is the sky parsed for those of us who fly in it? What are the invisible antechambers and corridors and waiting rooms for which there is a specific etiquette—napkins on your laps here, take off your shoes before entering there, no talking please? Here are some general rules, not enough to pass an FAA test but enough to get a sense of the architecture above, and how a pilot navigates it.

First, there is no such thing as sky without rules here in the United States. Even when someone tells you she can fly her drone below 400 feet without permission, this itself is a regulation. Remember that the highways and byways above are there

Maps

mostly to prevent aircraft collisions. Planes don't routinely cruise at 400 feet (the exceptions are helicopters working on, say, power lines, and, ahem, gyrocopters), so the drone is launchable, but it is still responsible for avoiding other aircraft. This is Class G airspace, considered "uncontrolled" and thus the most looseygoosey segment of the sky. Still, for a pilot sitting in a manned aircraft, it barks restrictions and mandates; for me, Class G extends from the ground to 1,200 feet, and I must nevertheless have one mile of visibility and stay clear of clouds. Class E starts at 1,200 feet. Required are three miles' visibility and the ability to skirt clouds by a margin of 1,000 feet above, 500 feet below, and 2,000 feet horizontally. This is just broad strokes: sometimes Class E airspace starts on the ground, sometimes at 700 feet instead of 1,200. Sometimes Class G goes all the way to 14,500 feet and then Class E starts. Yes, it gets confusing. All hail the mighty VFR sectional on my lap.

Class D, Class C, and Class B airspace are easier to understand: they surround increasingly busy airports, with mandates on how and when to talk to control towers, what avionics are needed to enter, the altitudes one must maintain, and the weather minimums. These airspace boundaries balloon on the sectionals in bright blue or magenta colors. They are festooned with tiny scribbled numbers and abbreviated instructions and acronyms and radio channels and elevations. These airspaces often crowd out our G and E airspace, claiming authority from the ground up.

There are restrictions over places like military bases and nuclear sites, but you can fly over most everything else without explicit permission as long as you are high enough. An altitude of 10,000 feet gets you over busy San Francisco International, for instance. The White House? You need to fly above 18,000 feet or military jets will be scrambled and on your tail in no time.

Why Fly

In India there is a structure called the Tower of Silence, where bodies are left to be consumed by vultures, part of a Parsi ritual called a sky burial. Here there is an airspace restriction that goes to "unlimited." No aircraft at any altitude within our troposphere may fly over this small circumference—a quietly touching affirmation that the departing soul deserves an unobstructed journey to its heaven. This tiny notation also tells a larger truth: so much is still unknown. But an aviator is well versed in wonder and mystery, so it is natural for us to err on the side of the metaphysical. Technology advances, and our avionics become more and more sensitive, but we can't yet detect an essence bound for the empyrean. Nor do we even know whether such an essence exists. Just in case, though, let's not get in its way.

It may surprise that there are so many unseen partitions above, but what sometimes catches me off guard is where the regulations lessen. I fly regularly over the Golden Gate Bridge, its cars like tiny matchbox racers, the waters below shimmering with sailboats and extreme currents. I bisect the towers, gaping right and left at their perfect posture, then I turn toward the hills again, the tiny faces of tourists perched at the various viewpoints upturned to this small yellow craft above them. Alcatraz sits calmly off to my right, the Coast Guard station at the base of the bridge in view on the left. As I approach the inlet to Sausalito, the body of the gyro is pummeled with invisible fists. This rumble is a meeting of rival gangs: the cold Pacific, the high hills, the narrowing inlet, and the warmer bay. I may linger in this sudden violence, curious about my own mettle or how the gyro handles, or I may decide *Enough* as I'm jerked and shoved. I will hit the throttle, quickly gain altitude, depart the melee, and head to Mount Tamalpais, whose reclining silhouette, recalling the outline of a sleeping Miwok princess, looms a little over 2,500 feet at its peak. Or I might turn back over the Marin headlands and follow the coast homeward, looking hopefully for the sparkle of a whale's blow catching the sunlight over a gingham sea.

When I first flew this Golden Gate Bridge lap, Paul sat in the back seat. He had so many more flying hours than me, and he routinely set flying challenges for himself (he has landed at an airport in all but one of California's fifty-eight counties); I asked if he would coach me through the flight. I kept muttering *Are you sure, are you sure?* as we approached, because this freedom seemed too good to be true. The Golden Gate Bridge! Don't we have to *ask permission*, I cried, like any good American used to the constant nannying of risk. An air traffic controller? An FAA official? File some sort of request? *Look at the chart*, Paul laughed, and indeed, it had already told me in its convoluted language of lines and numbers that as long as we had the right communication equipment (yes), flew under 3,000 feet (yes), and stayed at the required minimum safe altitudes over populated areas, we were (mostly) free to do as we pleased. But surely I had missed something. It seemed like an impossible stroke of good fortune, this sally over such an iconic landmark. It was like stepping into a museum and being told that it was okay to touch all the artifacts and sculptures and fabulous royal jewels.

Swinging out over the bay to set up for the approach was intimidating enough; then we crossed the bridge itself. My legs tingled and my stomach dropped as if I was looking over a cliff edge, and I had to do a little box breathing exercise to slow the adrenaline. I tried not to let Paul know I was wound so tightly, but my *Jeez, wow, oh boy* murmurs came clearly over the headset, and he assured me he had felt just as anxious on his inaugural bridge flight.

Similarly, I couldn't quite believe I was allowed to pilot the tiny open gyrocopter across the Sierra Nevada range, whose peaks can reach over 11,000 feet. As the sun began its ascent that morning in May, the temperatures were in the forties at my sea level home airport, so I wore heated gloves, two hats, a ski mask, and six layers of clothes under my winter flight suit to prepare for the mountain crossing. Paul had advised me to fly IFR, a tongue-in-cheek acronym that refers not to "instrument flying rules" but "I follow roads"—keep Interstate 50 underneath me, he said, *just in case*. Indeed, the mountains were white with recent snowfall and embowered on all sides, so an emergency landing there, while not impossible, would be hairy at best. There is a technique used to land in dense wood called "pancaking"; it involves flying as slowly as possible just over the treetops, then stalling the aircraft so that it falls flat like a pancake onto the upper branches. Sadly, it's not something you can really practice for, but the hope is that you've pancaked at such a perfect speed and with such calm and skill that you and your aircraft will gently nestle there, cradled by limbs and leaves. The reality is darker: you will most likely crash through the foliage toward earth and must simply pray that the tree itself will generously slow or stop your fall, and that you will avoid skewering by errant branches. The high-altitude conifers of the Sierras don't offer the leafy canopies that might make such a feat possible, but the (horrendous) option lurked in the back of my mind nevertheless.

Emergency tree landings haunt all kinds of pilots: I was once advised by a fellow paraglider to carry a cartridge of dental floss just in case, and when I looked puzzled, he explained that in the event one had no option but to land into a crown of trees, the thread, which was conveniently light and compact, also had the length necessary to reach the forest floor and any concerned rescuers there. A rope would then be tied to the dental floss, which you would haul up, loop around a branch, attach to your harness, and use to be lowered to the ground (I actually carried a belay device, so I could rappel down on my own). But landing in trees would be plan E on my Sierra crossing after (A) No troubles at all, (B) a convenient runway, (C) a long flattish field, (D) Route 50 itself. There was another reason Paul recommended IFR: since roads often reflect the path of least resistance through terrain, I could hopscotch between the highest peaks and stay at a mere 10,000 feet above sea level (I could go higher if necessary—my limit as a certified sport pilot in a gyrocopter is 10,000 feet mean sea level, except as needed to safely skirt ground below, whereupon I could take another 2,000 feet of altitude). In addition, if something did go wrong I would be landing relatively near a passing car or arriving emergency crews.

Mountain air currents are ferocious. As the day heats up, they worsen, so my plan was to cross as early as possible. On the other side waited the desert flatlands of Bishop, where I would stay for the night, heading to Death Valley the next day. A day after that, I would be high over the Grand Canyon, with a night among the red cliffs of Sedona, Arizona, and then Paul would meet me at an airport near Las Vegas to make the trip home himself.

Now I gaped at the whitened buttes, which marched in jagged fractals all the way to the horizon. My frozen cheeks were scrunched into a permanent grin, but I still managed to whisper, *You are flying over the Sierra, you are flying over the Sierra* as if to wake myself from a dream. What was I feeling? It was more complicated than joy, deeper than satisfaction, fuller than bravery. Honestly, I couldn't name what was washing over me, except that the jumble of emotions ultimately merged into one: awe. At one point I was so happily unmoored, and also nervous, that I began to take stock of my body, urging it to stay present in this most strange of perspectives. Wiggle the toes, flex the hamstrings, breathe out with the diaphragm, swallow once, feel the ears, feel the eyelids (heavy with cold), feel the top of the head, okay, you're here, you're good, you're above the Sierra at ten thousand feet, enjoy, celebrate, *you're doing this.*

When Belvin Maynard, an ordained minister and a test pilot during World War 1, flew his DH-4 biplane across the Sierra mountains during the final leg of the first transcontinental race in 1919, he had already been airborne for a few long days. (I fly no more than five or so hours a day during my own cross-country flights; Maynard probably flew twice that.) He had battled treacherous weather, landed at rudimentary airfields, fixed mechanical issues, and rested only at night. Exhausted, freezing cold, taut with anxiety, deafened by his roaring Liberty engine, he still managed to be gobsmacked by the landscape below. Of Lake Tahoe in particular, he later marveled how perfectly it sat "amid the tallest of the Sierras, with their peaks of silver white, as if some Divine hand might have placed it there, with the thought of perfect beauty."

Those who fly instrument flight rules (IFR) are subject to different regulations, many still obscure to me, a mere VFR pilot. These pilots can fly right into a cloud, reverting to the technology embedded in their panels to tell them whether they are still upright. This requires training and practice; once your sight is obstructed you cannot rely on your other senses—say, a falling stomach or the small bones in your ears—to tell you whether your plane is flying straight and level. Intuition, that praised sixth sense of grizzled television detectives, is of little use here, in IMC (pilots seem to love acronyms; this one stands for *instrument meteorological conditions*); you need either the horizon line outside or a fake one inside to stay upright and flying safely. None of this was known in the early days of flying. Mostly, pilots did not fly in bad weather (among other things, their wooden props would be quickly pecked to pieces by hard driving sleet) or at night. But when the air mail services started to push its pilots to fly continually, without regard to daylight or weather, pilots began mysteriously dying. This was shrugged off as a lack of good instincts and faltering decision-making skills.

Even VFR students, who are never supposed to lose external cues, are at some point put "under the hood," a device used to obscure vision outside the cockpit and which I remember as resembling a storm trooper helmet from the movie Star Wars when it was placed on my own head during my early Cessna flying lessons in 1981. The point is not just to underscore the efficacy of the instruments on your panel, but to put the fear of God in you, so that you realize how piss-poor your inner gyroscope is when it comes to a plane's orientation in the air. Your sightless body insists *this* is straight and level flight, even as the turn indicator tells you otherwise, and so the bank angle you've erroneously initiated becomes steeper. In the grip of spatial disorientation, you overcorrect wildly, and so it goes, you seesaw across the sky in an increasingly precarious floor routine until finally the instructor takes pity (or loses nerve) and grabs the controls.

The upshot of this training is that your breath comes in shallow gasps and you swear to yourself you will never go near a cloud bank or attempt to fly in marginal weather conditions, ever. Sadly, John F. Kennedy Jr. got himself into just this situation; he never fell afoul of visual flight rules, but nightfall (VFR allows night flying), heavy haze, and a dark ocean all conspired to obscure the horizon line outside his cockpit window anyway. Kennedy was a relatively inexperienced pilot without an

Why Fly

instrument rating, and he defaulted to his own inner proprioception once his visual cues failed him. He made the wrong corrections, struggled, overcorrected, struggled again. According to the data on the radar, in under two minutes he went into what NTSB investigators indelicately described later as a "graveyard spiral."

William Langewiesche reminded us just how tricky this situation can become when he wrote an article solely on the airplane's banked turn (called, aptly, "The Turn"). With visual cues we can orient our body to our brain to our position in relation to gravity and earth, but "if we then close our eyes, we have no way of telling that we are sitting at an angle . . . The airplane could be momentarily upside down and the passengers would not know." In a banked turn—in which the wings are at an angle to the horizon and the nose then turns—or even a very steep banked turn, a dropped pen will fall to the airplane's floor, not toward the earth over which you are tilted, possibly biting your lip and sucking in your breath. Only the steady sway of a pendulum can clue you in to the turn, because its momentum keeps the earth along its swing line. Myth says a pilot pulled out the chain of his pocket watch when his instruments failed him on a night flight to New York, saving hundreds of passengers.

It seems birds cannot fly without a horizon line either; Langewiesche describes two pilots from the 1930s obsessed with proving that neither inner resolve nor a strong biology can fly without a visible horizon; they threw blindfolded pigeons (pigeons again!) from their open cockpits, whereupon the poor birds spiraled to earth and died.

All this to say that while there are certainly natural pilots, as there are natural athletes (a famous air racer of the 1930s, Benny Howard, called this innate talent *go-grease*), ultimately IFR flying is a humbling exercise in ditching instinct and pinning your eyes to gyroscopic gauges that know better than you.

And so it is with life: go-grease is enough, until it isn't. Instincts are letting me down. The turn in my marriage is tightening; both of us are pulling on the stick wildly. The answer is to find the horizon line; but why can't we see it?

When someone dies unexpectedly the first question on our lips is *How did it happen?* But we don't say that out loud because it's prurient and unseemly. In the death of a marriage, no one has such hesitations. *How did it happen?* we ask greedily, as if one or two sentences can explain all those years. I understand this impulse, I too want the simple answer, those few words to pinpoint how our marriage is dying. Mortal combat? Suicide pact? Accident? Natural causes? Accordingly, I have sentences prepared for the inevitable inquisition: We want different things. We stopped building something together. We take each other for granted. We've grown apart.

Any or all of those are true, but toward the end it is the sudden symptoms that are easier to explain. Verbal sparring. Less time spent doing fun things. Less sex. More resentment. No time doing fun things. Then the affection starts to go, and then Hail Mary sex, then *That was so good why don't we have more of that,* then more resentment, less affection, and so the cycle continues. There are instruments to look at, a way to regain our horizon, but we pin our eyes outside anyway. We stare where we think the horizon should be and down, down we go, a graveyard spiral.

18

The Controls

The 122nd Composite Air Group was reluctantly signed into being by Stalin in October 1941 as the Nazis were laying siege to Leningrad and the Russians were desperate for pilots. "Reluctantly," because the order signified a groundbreaking change to military protocol. The 122nd, it turns out, was an all-female combat unit. Made up mostly of teens and those in their early twenties, these two hundred women were given only a few months to learn flight, navigation, combat strategy, and aircraft maintenance. The 122nd was then divided into the 586th Fighter Regiment, the 587th Bomber Regiment, and the 588th Air Regiment. Of these three units, two joined male counterparts. Only the 588th remained all-female. Because of this, it was assigned to fly the absurdly underpowered and underequipped Polikarpov Po-2.

The Po-2 was a *biplane*, built in 1927, made of wood and canvas and bereft of any defensive weapons, radios, or radar. It was a wondrously slow and flimsy aircraft to be flying into battle, but the top command reasoned that good equipment was best saved for male pilots and wasted on women. And so the Po-2, once used as a crop duster, was now pressed into duty as a combat plane against the best technology of the time: the fighter aircraft of the Nazi Luftwaffe.

The Po-2 cruised at barely 70 miles per hour with a top speed of 93. This lack of power meant that after the bombs were loaded, one under each wing, the two women on board could not wear parachutes or carry any armaments. In addition, without radios or radar, they held paper maps on their laps with frostbitten fingers and peered through frozen lashes while the Russian winter wind howled through their open cockpit. The wood and canvas fuselage of the Po-2 also offered no protection against strafing and easily caught fire. As if this wasn't perilous enough, the pilots were to fly in the dead of night, drop low over heavily armed German encampments on the front lines, and release explosives meant mostly to keep German soldiers from sleep, but also to maim and to kill. Picture this: young, inexperienced pilots aboard sluggish relics, lurching into sweeping searchlights, heavy ground artillery, and the paths of sleek Messerschmitt fighters that catapulted across the sky at almost 400 miles per hour. Surely this was a disaster. The women of the 588th were mere fodder in a larger, desperate Russian campaign.

In fact, the 588th was a master class in daring and determination and ultimate success. It was also a master class in what is important when it comes to flight itself, which is often not the fancy avionics or the top speeds or the newest wing designs.

The 588th flew not in formation, but in one long line, three minutes apart, all through the night. The approaching pilot throttled back her engines at 4,000 feet, then pointed the nose downward in a dive to become a quiet, deadly arrow. The wind whistling through the wing wires greatly unnerved the Germans below, maybe even more than the two bombs that would explode soon after, released by the navigator over the target at 2,000 feet. Soon enough the charred bodies pried from downed Po-2s revealed that the Russian pilots were women. This, along with the certainty that the diving planes sounded like sweeping brooms, meant that the anxious, sleep deprived soldiers soon gave their attackers the nickname *Nachthexen*, or Night Witches.

Over time the Night Witches grew combat savvy, developing a strategy of flying in twos, with one pilot purposefully diverting into the unholy beams of light to draw fire while the other descended quickly with her bombs. Sometimes a bomb would "stick and not drop," remembers Major Irina Rakobolskaya. Midflight, "the navigator would get out of the cockpit, stand on the wing, and reach down with her hands to push it loose." But the timing was vital: they could not bomb at too low an altitude, because the explosion could ignite the delicate Po-2 itself.

Navigator Yevgeniya Zhigulenko remembers another hazard of the trade: when caught in a German searchlight a pilot was temporarily blinded. Unable to see a horizon, she often became disoriented, and her Po-2 might stall or simply plow into the unseen terrain.

And so it went in one grim loop: lowering cloud ceilings, darkness, searchlights, the heat of dropped bombs, the menace of the Messerschmitts, the arcing lights of ground artillery. Keeping this regular tempo was dangerous for the Night Witches, but flight command insisted: constant bombardment was the only way to wear down the enemy. The 588th regularly flew between eight and eighteen sorties before the sun came up.

Why Fly

The Night Witches lived up to their name: their success seemed like sorcery. Indeed, the small Po-2 had an uncanny invisibility, its nonmetal frame and low cruising altitude allowing it to evade German radar. Spookier still was how the Po-2 could almost magically shake off its high-tech pursuers. But it wasn't magic, it was physics: the top speed of the Po-2 was lower than the stall speed of the Messerschmitts and Focke-Wulfs that chased them. A Night Witch could escape a German combat plane with a sudden turn, whereupon the Luftwaffe aircraft risked a fall from the sky if it tried to slow enough to keep pace. Ultimately the Nazis' superior technology could fly proverbial circles around the antiquated design of the Po-2, but those circles were ineffective.

The Night Witches flew for the next four years. They dropped 23,000 tons of bombs on German targets, destroying bodies, equipment, sleep, morale. Enemy troops on the ground and in the air were both incensed and frightened to be outmaneuvered by *women*, who showed such proficiency that rumors soon circulated that Night Witches were being given injections "to give us a feline's perfect vision at night," remembers Nadezhda Popova, a Night Witch pilot who flew 852 missions and was later named a Hero of the Soviet Union.

Anne Noggle interviewed the Soviet women who flew in World War II and compiled those extensive transcriptions in her book *A Dance with Death*. Decorated Night Witch Marina Chechneva told Noggle how male peers were not supportive of her flying career even before the war. She laments how they repeatedly told her, "'Aviation is not a woman's affair,' . . . and tried in every possible way to dissuade women from joining the Air Club." Yes, Russia had formally declared women legal equals to men in 1917 (the first country to do so), but culturally, this proclamation was not upheld; Popova recounts the resistance of the military to female combat pilots, and it dismayed her that "no one in the armed services wanted to give women the freedom to die."

All the regiments of the 122nd Composite Air Group quickly proved their mettle, but the higher-ups in the Soviet military mostly ignored or belittled their contributions. It was no wonder, then, that Lieutenant Colonel Valentin Markov, assigned to the 587th bomber regiment after the death of their leader, Marina Raskova, assumed that his female aviators would be subpar and his task difficult. He quickly saw the opposite: they "never whimpered, they never complained, and they were very courageous."

When the war ended, the aircraft opportunities in civilian life were given to the male pilots, much to the chagrin of the women who had fought so valiantly, against such odds. Back to menial jobs and housewifery went the dazzling 122nd Composite Air Group. "Almost all of these women were shot down, and after hospitalization they came back to the regiment and flew bravely," Lt. Col. Markov told Noggle of his unit for *Dancing with Death*. Yet, "very few of my girls were awarded that highest title [Hero of the Soviet Union]. If I could turn time back, I would have promoted many more of them for that award. Now I have a very grave sentiment about that, because many of them deserved it."

Navigation

In the early 1990s, I volunteered as a ranger on North America's highest mountain, Denali. My job was to ski around base camp and pick up trash left by exhausted climbing teams, assist with medical issues, help with rescues. One day a call came in that a small plane had gone down in the mountains. The skies were blue, "the mountains" clearly nearby, but the helicopter pilot shook his head and said there was no chance we were finding it. White plane, he said. White snow. With the earnestness of a city slicker who knew little about Alaska, I responded, "I have great eyesight, I think we will."

In my tiny defense, we had flown in on a cloudy day, and we would fly out on one, so no wonder I had not fully understood. Yes, I had been skiing for days on Denali's flanks, privy to the high peaks all around, themselves stupefying in their grandeur but somehow still kept in check by the hard sky against them. But now, as the helicopter rose off the glacier, I sucked in my

Why Fly

breath. It was as if someone had slapped me hard across the face. Mountains surged in every direction like ripples on an ocean. For hundreds of miles, stretched out beneath our skids like a drawn-out dirge, ran endless crenellations, blinding white, stopping only at the horizon line. It was the equivalent of the night sky as seen from your back in the grass far from city lights, how the sight disorients and even frightens, how the more you stare and the more stars you make out and the deeper into the black you go the less comprehension you feel. That day in the helicopter my senses were struck dumb, and all I was left with was a deeply visceral sense of the meaning of "lost." We dutifully flew our paltry search pattern. I stared and stared until my eyes watered. The plane was never found.

. . .

Pilots use many navigation techniques to keep from getting truly lost. One is called "dead reckoning," and entails calculations throughout the flight of compass heading, elapsed time, airspeed, wind speed, and wind direction. The beauty of dead reckoning is that it needs no external beacons or waypoints, and visual contact with the ground is irrelevant. The difficulty is that it demands strenuous multitasking. No wonder in the early days of postal flight, pilot James Hill opted for a simpler dead reckoning technique when in bad weather he would light a cigar as he took off from Cleveland, and by the time it was a stub singeing his fingers, he guessed that somewhere below the clouds lay his mail stop of Bellefonte, Pennsylvania.

A more sophisticated form of dead reckoning is described by Mark Vanhoenacker in his book *Skyfaring, A Journey with a Pilot*, in which an onboard navigation system called *inertial navigation* continually logs the twists and turns and speed changes of the plane itself. By calculating its own rotations and accelerations it always knows its place over the world, and takes much if not all of the navigational burden off of the pilot.

The term "dead reckoning" is not derived from the word "dead," but from "ded," a shortening of "deduced." Yet the average Joe often uses the term incorrectly while boasting of his wild adventure and successful navigation through it because, let's face it, calling it *dead reckoning* has an edgy, stand-at-the-helm-judging-the-shoals element, that galloping-your-horse-to-the-next-town-where-your-sheriff-justice-is-needed feel. But in using time, airspeed, distance, and direction numbers you resemble more a nerdy academic than the tousled-hair-cleft-in-the-chin hero. For that look, you are most likely using what aviators call *pilotage*.

"Pilotage" refers to pinpointing your location by matching land features outside the cockpit with those on a map. It's not even that heroic; it's basically what your grandparents did when they snatched the AAA maps made of paper from the glove compartment of the family station wagon (where there may also have actually been gloves) and snapped them open en route. The person in the passenger seat sang out highway exits and road names. Fingers were snaked along blue lines, black lines, intersections. Landmarks and signage on the ground were matched to the map and vice versa. And somehow the destination was always reached with little or no delay or error—or maybe it was just that delay and error were expected and not noticed as they would be today, because today most of us rely almost exclusively on a new form of navigation that has mostly banished delay and error, which is GPS.

Pilotage also has limits; it becomes useless in bad weather when a pilot's view of the ground is obscured. This can be a nuisance, or it can be fatal. During World War I, entire squadrons lost their way over cloud cover, became low on fuel, and made forced landings in enemy territory. Descending to identify ground features meant flying within reach of artillery fire, so that wasn't an option. Still, flying in peacetime with clear weather did not guarantee safety either. This was because ground maps of the early twentieth century, already inaccurate for the layman, failed completely for a pilot. Ground maps depict two-dimensional space—fine for driving on roads, but those in the air need a three-dimensional understanding. Street names are of little use; it is large landmarks like lakes and towns that matter. It's the height of mountains. It's the direction of railroads.

When I first began flying lessons in 1981, there were no fancy avionics, and I was taught to navigate using both dead reckoning and pilotage in tandem. I calculated where I was on the map using a slide rule and compass and pencil and the sectional on my lap while also looking out the window for railways and lakes and large power plants. Meanwhile, one also had to keep the plane straight and level. And constantly recalculate drift based on shifting wind directions and speeds (also assessed only by more math). No wonder it took all I had to hop a little Cessna 152 from place to place in those early days, making flying the hardest thing I had ever tackled until then, no doubt. These days GPS has changed all that. Navigation is so much easier. I sometimes miss the uncertainty that accompanied reading paper maps on road trips by car and the serendipity and unforeseen adventure that ensued, but when it comes to flight I remain eternally grateful for the advent of GPS in the cockpit.

It strikes me that we often take stock of our own life using both dead reckoning and pilotage. We flourish the map of our past, lay it flat on our lap, and do the calculations: this decision placed me here, and then I sped forward for a while until I changed lovers/jobs/cities and off I went over the treacherous mountains of this, the choppy air currents of that. The porpoising of adolescence, the straightaway of midlife, the people to whom we veered for love or friendship. And now here we are, not just in this financial situation, with that partner, these kids, that career, but at this particular juncture, on our own inner topography. This is not just *where* we are, but *who* we are.

. . .

When the first transcontinental air race kicked off in 1919, each pilot was given a map devised by the U.S. Postal Service. It was simply a ground map reprinted on paper that could be unrolled incrementally during flight, making it easier to read in the biplane's open cockpit. "The issued maps were very good except for the lack of mountains," one participant remarked dryly. This is why in the early years it was not uncommon for a pilot to resort to the most ancient of wayfinding techniques: land in a farmer's field and ask for directions.

This first transcontinental race exposed more than the pitiful state of aeronautical charts. Despite birthing the Wright Flyer and introducing a viable plane to the world, the United States had quickly dropped well behind Europe in aviation. Countries overseas had experienced firsthand the airplane's potential as a weapon of war, when it was first used for unarmed reconnaissance in the early days of World War I. Initially, opposing pilots gave each other amiable salutes from the cockpits. As the fighting continued and technology improved, this practice morphed into what John Lancaster describes in his book *The Great Air Race* as "plinking at each other with sidearms and rifles." With the arrival of synchronizing machine guns that could shoot through

Why Fly

a spinning propeller came the bitter aerial dogfight. Also soon implemented: rudimentary bombing campaigns.

Postwar Europeans were now busy envisioning aviation's peacetime uses—several commercial airlines were in place by 1920, including a London-to-Paris route using converted Farman F-60 bombers. Meanwhile, the U.S. government, late to the overseas fight and so mostly dismissive of the airplane's potential, was yet to be convinced. Congress did not believe commercial aviation had a future, and the military's Air Service arm was underfunded. Meanwhile few private manufacturers were making aircraft or equipment. Overall demand was lackluster.

After all, most Americans understood flying to be strange and full of peril. In a classic chicken-and-egg scenario, it didn't help that infrastructure was threadbare. No radio beacons were in use yet, though the technology had been invented in 1902. Airfields were scarce, refueling options difficult, weather forecasting inaccurate.

The tug-of-war began: those who believed flying was dangerous and unreliable and not worth an investment of time, money, or creativity pulled against those who despaired that further stalling would tank America's future as an economic and military power.

Into this fray comes the U.S. Postal Service. Again.

We think of the USPS as antiquated, an analog institution in a digital world. Paper! Pens! Its most recent advancements are postal boxes with tamper-proof mail slots and stamps that no longer must be licked. Large metal containers on various corners! Yet over a century ago the U.S. Postal Service was full of forward thinkers; it had invented the preflight checklist, remember; later, its mailbag snagging system would greatly influence those glider takeoff techniques in World War II. And as early as 1911 it began to imagine that these new machines

Navigation

called airplanes could become part of its mail delivery system. At first, "air mail" endured many failures (mailbags thrown from cockpits that burst on impact, lost pilots, inclement weather, fatalities) but finally a reliable New-York-to-Chicago route was established, opening in phases starting in May 1919. Letters began to arrive within seven hours instead of the fourteen hours when delivered by train, and buoyed by this success, postmaster Otto Praeger set his sights on crossing all 2,700 or so miles of the country. His plan: a relay system of planes, much like the Pony Express of yore (the Pony Express was established in 1860, and despite its resonance in myth and history, it lasted only a year and a half before it went bankrupt). Unbeknownst to him, another dreamer, Brigadier General Billy Mitchell, was about to announce his own bold vision for cross-country flight, meant to prove an airplane's worth as well as to ignite civilian and congressional support for American aviation: an air race from San Francisco to New York.

This first air race was formally named "the Reliability and Endurance Test." The hope was that the public could be convinced of aviation's safety and wowed by its efficiency and pizzazz. Billy Mitchell announced his idea in September 1919 and then realized his weather window for the year was rapidly closing and so, incredibly, planned the cross-country race for a month hence. He leveraged the might of the Air Service, sending soldiers to implore townspeople from coast to coast to quickly grade fields and bring in airplane supplies. Runways were carved from any open land—some were dangerously situated in weird bowls, with hazards on all sides, which from a non-pilot point of view surely seemed perfectly adequate. Fuel, nuts, spare propellers, tires, bolts, and tools were lugged to each of the twenty stops. Crudely drawn maps that showed the next leg of the race were prepared for the incoming pilots. So tight was the schedule that some runways were not even complete by the time of the race's start and others lacked crucial supplies.

Today I can make a four-day trip in my gyrocopter, finding safe places every hour and a half on which to land and rest and refuel as necessary (I sometimes see two small airports within a few miles of each other.) For this I have the Reliability and Endurance Test to thank. As Lancaster notes in *The Great Air Race*, "More important to the development of aviation in America, the race had spawned a series of airfields at about 200-mile intervals across the U.S." Even if many of those fields may no longer remain, the infrastructure they started, as well as the excitement about flight they kept alive, make the airfields I do land on these days their cherished descendants. But back in 1919, this future remained uncertain.

These first transcontinental pilots faced many threats. Some were forced to the ground by terrible weather, others by mechanical difficulty. Wrecked planes were quickly strewn across mountains and boggy fields, and by the second day, four lives had been lost. An editorial in the *Buffalo Express* noted that the air race seemed to be killing at the rate of a wartime sortie. "Is the game worth such sacrifices?" it fumed. "Could not the quality of airplanes be adequately tested without contests that involve the lives of so many brave men?" In the ensuing days pilots would make emergency landings regularly. Leaking radiators, empty fuel tanks, propellers quickly gnawed into useless stubs by driving rain were all reasons to pick a field (or in one case a large lake) and attempt a safe return to earth. Pilots slept in snowbanks, farmhouses, cornfields. They guarded against voracious souvenir hunters who stole vital parts like radiator caps. They beat off hogs eager to chew at their canvas fuselages.

The Reliability and Endurance Test would eventually claim nine lives, but its intended goal of spreading the gospel of aviation worked. It helped that the winner of the race was the ordained minister Belvin Maynard, who flew with his dog Trixie and an able mechanic, earning the catchy nickname the Flying Parson. He made it across the country in three days, six hours, 16 minutes, and 47 seconds. Within the year the postal service had laid its own transcontinental route between New York and San Francisco. By 1921 mail would be delivered come rain, shine, snow, or dark of night in a day and a half, a full three days ahead of a train.

By the mid-1930s the government began to make it easier to fly across the country without getting hopelessly lost. They hired pilots to identify barns with roofs big enough to mark the name of nearby towns in large letters, signaling upward to pilots where they were on the landscape. Air marking, as the job was called, was one of the few occupations a woman could get, and the roster of air markers included the pioneering aviators Louise Thaden and Blanche Noyes; Noyes later became head of the air marking division. One pilot, lost in a storm and low on fuel, remembers "the July afternoon in the 1950s when an American barn may have saved my life. For our safe landing, we were thankful for Blanche Noyes."

Today there are no large letters emblazoned on roofs. There are, however, invisible flags planted as numeric coordinates that show up on aerial instrument maps. These five-letter designations dot the planet, and often trumpet something about the ground on which they stand—ANCOR is near the harbor town of Perth, Australia, TULIP lies off Holland, and in basketball-proud Houston, SSLAM is a few miles from DUUNK. Near my own small airport lies Charles M. Schulz–Sonoma County

Why Fly

Airport, named after the artist who drew the famous *Peanuts* comic strip (and the yellow bird in it for which our gyro is named, Woodstock); a plane on instrument flight rules might use waypoint PIGPN to land on its 32 runway, or SNUPY when approaching from the east.

These days I have no updated map for my current life, no beacon (MARRG? DIVRC?) that pinpoints my destination. On the surface the terrain is familiar—my home, my neighborhood—but its emotional landscape has become increasingly vast and baffling. Yet to be truly lost, you must know where you want to be and see that you aren't there. I do not yet have those coordinates; I wish it were that easy.

Pilots file flight plans with the FAA specifying their intentions—*This is the airport I will land at and when I will be there*—and if they don't cancel the plan upon arrival, brows are creased, calls are made, and the pilot apologizes for forgetting. The pilot was lost to everyone except himself. But sometimes the pilot is lost-lost, not at his intended destination and not reachable by his phone. Somewhere an emergency locator transmitter is sounding, an airtag is quietly beeping, a smartphone is calling out its location, and satellites are triangulating, and then a search begins.

PART 6

FLIGHT (INBOUND)

Every time I have gone up on an airplane . . . I have had the consciousness of a great new discovery. "I see," I have thought. "This was the idea. And now I understand everything."

ISAK DINESEN

Weather

On day two of my cross-country gyrocopter trip, with the high Sierra behind me, I set my sights on Death Valley. I was planning a morning departure from the Bishop, California, airfield on which I'd landed the afternoon before, betting that an early start would reward me with relatively calm air. But as I arrived at the small airfield, crosswinds were caterwauling at 22 mph, swinging wildly, with peak gusts of 33 mph. This was well over the parameters of a safe takeoff for me, and being uncertain of what this also meant for my journey ahead, I waited.

I gazed at the windsock with longing. I did another walk-around of the gyrocopter. I watched the local birds in flight. They dipped and pirouetted, allowed themselves to be pushed backward for a moment, then feinted sideways, headed fast downwind, and turned again. They appeared to be playing, and why not, they had nowhere they needed to be, no narrow valley to negotiate, no high mountains to cross, no hotel booked. I

Why Fly

turned my back on the avian frolic and instead dialed nearby airports to listen intently to their automated weather reports, then tried to build some sort of mental model of the hope/despair that might lie along my route. Meanwhile the flight chart on my tablet was colored an orange-yellow to signify *moderate turbulence*. "Moderate" sounds harmless, and indeed the FAA defines it as "changes in attitude/altitude but the aircraft remains in positive control at all times." Positive control! That's good news. But these guidelines apply to much bigger planes, which becomes clear when they explain that "Occupants feel definite strains against seat belts or shoulder straps. Unsecured objects are dislodged. Food service and walking are difficult." Moderate turbulence for a light, small, underpowered, open aircraft like mine? Not so moderate.

I walked inside the pilot shack, less a shack than a one-level cement square with an office vibe, and said hello to the local flight school instructors who were canceling the morning flights and gazing at the windsock too. Then we engaged in a familiar ritual: we earnestly predicted what the winds would do, even though talking about it didn't change a thing. Despite our convoluted assessments, our pensive retelling of past weather conditions on days just like this, and our stream of hopeful numbers, the simple answer remained *Shitshow until further notice*.

The chances that the winds would abate in the afternoon were pretty much nil, but still I waited. A helicopter crew working on utility lines along an eastern mountain range walked in. The pilot asked if that was my yellow gyro on the tarmac and pronounced it *Very cool*. I asked him how conditions were out there. His rotorcraft was highly powered, a completely different beast than mine, and he said he wasn't sure what mine could handle, then concurred, *Rock and roll. But maybe it'll die down?*

Pilots like to give each other hope. The alternative is to declare oneself grounded and settle for an earthbound day. Better to wait it out, a pilot would agree.

I sat back down in a chair and looked at my maps. I planned out alternate routes. I asked the locals for more insider knowledge. Talk that had sounded terrifying to me just a little earlier started to sound par for the course: the way the rushing wind compressed down the valley, the mechanical turbulence triggered by high mountain ranges both east and west of me, the airport runways on which I could land for refuge, the pilots who might offer me a corner of their hangar. Three hours turned to four. In that time, my view of what conditions were acceptable to fly in began to slip. I had arrived ready to take off in a quartering wind of 10 miles per hour with no wind gusts, but that soon morphed into under 15 miles per hour with gusts of 23 as long as they came right down the runway. Another hour and a half passed. I decided a steady 20 miles per hour straight down the runway was just fine. I called Paul for his insight. Gusting to thirty-three was a no go, but twenty straight down, sure. But then what was ahead? More musing. More guessing. More inane attempts at future prediction. It wasn't just the takeoff, after all. There would be a whole day of wind conditions at varying altitudes and temperatures over different obstacles once in flight.

It's worth saying that these winds had not been in the forecast even the day before, and as climate change worsens, these kinds of surprises will occur with more frequency. Yet I still marvel at the accuracy we do have. Pilots along treacherous mail routes in the early days of aviation were not so lucky. They often found themselves in appalling weather conditions without warning and were forced to reckon with options that ranged from bad to worse. The pilot Antoine de Saint-Exupéry

Why Fly

was hit suddenly by terrible turbulence on a bluebird day over Patagonia in the early 1930s. He writes with convoluted flair of how he soon found himself five miles out to sea, "spat . . . by a monstrous cough, vomited out of my valley as from the mouth of a howitzer." For the next hour and a half, he and his biplane tried in vain to make headway back to the coast. He fought 150 mph headwinds and repeated downdrafts that shoved him perilously close to the heaving ocean. He lost feeling in his hands, and gained only 200 feet over forty minutes. At some point the ribs of his wings began to separate, his storage batteries were thrown against the ceiling, and the wing cables strained so badly that they were "sawed down to the last thread." If the FAA had been around at the time, it would have called this *extreme turbulence*, a stage worse than even *severe turbulence*. This was turbulence "in which the aircraft is violently tossed about and is practically impossible to control. It may cause structural damage." There is no worse turbulence than this, but even then the FAA offers hope. The aircraft isn't impossible to control, it is *practically impossible to control*. The turbulence won't destroy your craft, *it may cause structural damage*. Indeed, Saint-Exupéry escapes the hell and lands his embattled plane safely, but he cannot utter a word to the ground crew. "I climbed out of the cockpit and walked off. There was nothing to say . . . I had no grip on what I'd been through . . . You cannot convey things to people by piling up adjectives, by stammering."

In the early afternoon the winds began to abate. It wasn't a Saint-Exupéry miracle like the one related above, but it still felt like divine benediction. At two o'clock, after seven hours at the airport, the windsock stopped spasming and the automated weather system reported 13 miles per hour straight down the runway with gusts of 18. After what I'd seen, this seemed heavenly. But how did the weather here translate to the rest of my route, as the desert narrowed and the temperatures to the south rose? I decided it was worth it to find out. I zipped up my flight suit, bade my new pilot friends farewell, braced myself for howitzer coughs, and took off without a hitch.

If you've flown for as long as I have in one area—almost twenty-five years at my airport—you notice changes. What was once a viable emergency landing option in case of engine trouble on takeoff is now a mall/sports field/parking lot. Along the base of a nearby mountain, new mansions appear every few years, ascending the hills like the slowest of rock climbers. The invisible owners limn their property with vineyards and bright blue pools and sometimes a tennis court, and I watch the landscaped trees grow taller and wider, ultimately shielding the houses from neighbors but never from me. In a nearby town an abandoned military airfield still shows the outlines of its huge runways, but slowly a development has carved cul-de-sacs and plopped identical square homes on what was once the ramp, the taxiway, the hold short line, the first half of the runway itself. The tarmac that does remain has decayed into a geometric pattern of cracks and crumbles that from the air reminds of some ancient sleeping reptile, its squamation a strange mimic, or maybe mockery, of the suburban grid pattern that will, in the coming years, completely overtake it.

Meanwhile a small military town on a swampy expanse does the opposite. It molts into the ground, roofs sagging inward, a tennis court growing mossy. When I first flew over it, it looked intact, and I assumed it was a bustling little enclave. It had a pretty tree-lined road leading into it, and a beveled fishing dock over the surrounding stream. But a low, slow pass, unique to the lovely experimental aircraft I fly, revealed that no one was there and hadn't been for a while. Over the years this place shed itself quietly, and then there was a long period when I didn't skim over it anymore, pulled to new places. The first time I returned I circled and circled wondering if I had imagined it all. It was gone, bulldozed to the ground and cleared and left to nature. All I could make out were a few blurring squares of concrete pad. I might have thought I was crazy, but the shaggy trees in an unnatural line remained, a reminder that a human-made road had once been here and had led to that now vanished hamlet.

There were other, more disturbing changes. Leopard sharks no longer gathered in the bay. I saw fewer and fewer dolphins near the shoreline; in recent years I've seen none. The tiny minnow shape of seals has also waned. Whole mountainsides are now bereft of any visible wildlife, no matter how closely I peer.

But mostly what I've noticed is the wind.

Weather irregularities came into view only recently for most people. But as a pilot I could tell that something was changing long before. Twenty years ago, the expected "glass-off" at dusk began to disappear. Glass-off is the period when the wind leaves its afternoon bluster behind, easing to a gentle breeze, making water smooth as glass and pilots who have certain wind requirements very happy. Now the winds would stay high past dark. A few years later the calm winds at dawn that I could always count on also began to disappear. It was as if I was in some scary B movie and one by one the parameters I needed in order to fly safely were being picked off by mysterious forces. I would wake before sunrise, call the automated weather system at the airport, and be surprised by an eight-knot breeze instead of the assuring *Winds calm* that usually greeted me. It wasn't that I couldn't fly my trike in eight knots, but it meant that the wind would likely be increasing quickly as temperatures changed; my morning flight under a hang glider wing would be spent fighting wind shear and rising turbulence. Paul didn't like the rising turbulence either; he eventually stopped flying his own trike, opting for Woodstock's narrow overhead rotor blades that barely register rough air.

When I lamented the changing conditions to pilots of bigger planes, their reaction was mostly a shrug and a declaration that they had not really noticed. And why should they have noticed—they didn't need consider the same narrow wind requirements for their own sky adventures. Then I started to mumble about *climate weirding, climate chaos, climate emergency* to non-pilots, who would look at me with puzzlement and what they hoped was sympathy. The crisis wasn't yet showing up in their day-to-day lives. Then: drought, flooding, ferocious hurricane seasons, monster wildfires. It all began squalling into public consciousness. Thick smoke from megafires, homes lost to flames, and whispers of the inability to insure a house deemed sitting on too-precarious terrain became routine. As I write this, what once might have been a containable Southern California fire took hold in vegetation parched by eight months of no rain. It was then scooped up and thrown about by incredible 100-mile-per-hour winds. The result is the destruction of thousands of homes by fire, the densely packed communities of Pacific Palisades and Altadena now just a smoldering landscape of naked chimneys and concrete pads.

And what of the commercial flights, landing with food scattered from dispensary carts, fresh dents in their ceilings from luggage thrown about, and passengers who emerge nursing bruises or worse? I wasn't happy to hear these stories, but I felt a teeny bit vindicated, and not at all surprised. These planes are encountering what is called "clear air turbulence," a high-altitude phenomenon of violent air currents that are hard to see on radar because they lack moisture, and which have worsened because of climate change. Recent studies claim that between 1979 and 2020, clear air turbulence has increased by 55 percent and, scientists predict, will at least triple the 1979 figures by the end of the century. Remember when Captain Steve Allright assured phobic flyers that turbulence was not dangerous? He is correct for the moment; turbulence is almost never (I say "almost never" instead of "never," but mostly I mean "never") extreme enough to severely damage or overpower a huge commercial jet, especially when it is at a high enough altitude. After all, it is not turbulence that is generally the problem, but the ground that rises to meet us before we can correct for the disruption. This is the danger of a microburst encountered on, say, approach to land, though we now have technology that identifies microbursts so they can be avoided. As I reminded my wife, we routinely fly research planes into actual hurricanes. But in the Anthropocene, as we hurl increasing amounts of methane and CO_2 skyward at our delicate atmosphere, we are entering unknown territory. It's fair for you to simply check back later for updates from Captain Allright as the temperature of the earth elevates and the turbulence responds in kind.

Up in my gyro, approaching the Owens Valley of eastern California, I was steeled for a messy trip. But again I was in luck; the wind gods spared me. Later I defined the conditions to Paul as "sporty," with a low corresponding fear factor. It helped that my bar for what constituted difficult and fear-inducing had changed since just yesterday. I was now a gyro pilot who had flown over the Sierra. I was now a gyro pilot who had flown out of the Bishop airport. I was now a gyro pilot who had flown in afternoon desert winds. But I also knew that this was a dangerous moment. Not because of the conditions, but because of the mindset that came with it. I was trying to find my outer envelope but not push beyond what I was ready for. It was a delicate balance, honed from years of other adventures in my life: first descents by whitewater raft on unexplored rivers, bikepacking through steep, empty landscapes, big city firefighting, paraglider flights over all kinds of terrain. Years of learning from my mistakes.

Could I cross the cattle grate on my all-terrain electric skateboard, I once wondered, deciding *yes*, especially if I picked up speed. *No* would have been the better answer (but I survived uninjured).

If the surf report says triple overhead, but it doesn't look to you from the beach like triple overhead, is it smart to get into the water on your board "just for a workout"? *Yes*, I told myself. *No* was the right answer (but I paddled out and back uninjured).

These days, sharpened by experience, wiser with age, I am a risk assessment machine. You're still a dummy with too much education and too little street sense, I remind myself. I pay attention to details. I don't pick and choose which ones suit me; I take them all into account. I always have a plan B, and a plan C. I don't let myself be rushed. If there's an inflection point, I err on the side of the easier/safer/boring/cowardly story rather than hero/gnarly/riskier/bragging rights version. I check my motivations. Trying to prove something or trying to learn something? "When in doubt, chicken out," some pilot said at one point to someone, somewhere. Also, the famous saw: "There are old pilots. There are bold pilots. But there are no old bold pilots."

Aviators on mail routes flew regularly into severe blizzards, heavy rains, and whiteouts. They endured derechos and high mountain winds with little certainty whether they and their rudimentary aircraft could survive the beating; they were often the first to experience these conditions in a plane. Even as the years rolled on and the science solidified around lift and weight, thrust and drag, still the outer limits were pushed. (This tendency is called *risk homeostasis*. We may improve safety in, say, car braking systems, but studies show that we then drive faster, so the risk remains the same.)

It was the "Hump" pilots of World War II who arguably experienced the most treacherous flying conditions in the world. The Hump was what pilots called the Burma-China route over which they ferried supplies to waiting troops. Maps of the area were incomplete, weather forecasting was minimal, high Himalayan peaks jutted upward, merciless jungle lay below.

"As long as the wings are level, an airplane is well mannered and slow to anger," reminds the writer William Langewiesche, but this observation was of little use to Hump pilots; 100-miles-per-hour winds routinely ambushed their aircraft, and it was not unusual for a storm to descend without warning, or for a film of ice six inches thick to suddenly coat the windshield and the propellers, leading to loss of lift and a bailout or a crash. Hump pilots didn't have the routine luxury of level wings; they instead battled an aircraft piqued repeatedly into unholy tantrums.

Yet even these experienced fliers were gobsmacked by the weather that arrived one January night. As Caroline Alexander explains in her book *Skies of Thunder*, Hump pilots were "not flying so much as being hurled." Maydays were exploding on the radio, jamming frequencies. Pilots who had been flying for twenty years had never seen such abominable conditions. Winds not only hit 200 miles per hour but came from all directions and shifted abruptly, ferocious and unrelenting. Downdrafts cudgeled powerful C-46s, dropping them three thousand feet even as they maxed out their engines. "Then just as suddenly we were propelled upward at 4,000 ft per minute right on through our assigned altitude to 22,000 feet ... we were having trouble keeping the airplane right side up." Dreaded ice collected on wings and windshields and clogged engines. Pilots with no bearings or instruments and subject to such vertiginous drops in altitude had no way of knowing whether they would suddenly slam into a Himalayan mountainside (many did). Punched off course, unable to lock onto beacons, often barely maintaining controlled flight, planes were lost in frightening territory. One pilot described a series of terrifying assaults by the weather, only to say "Then things really began to happen." He went on, "Suddenly we were on our back. While hanging in my safety belt and with the dirt from the floor falling all around, I realized it would be impossible to bail out. The copilot and I fought the controls until we finally righted the ship at 21,000 feet."

It comes as no surprise that 594 transport planes were lost over the Hump, with a loose estimate of 1,659 to 3,861 soldiers killed or missing. Incredibly, twelve hundred men were thought to have survived bailouts, often walking for weeks through jungle or wading in waist-high snow across Himalayan peaks.

Even now, with so much more understanding of flight parameters, such better instruments, and hardier aircraft, most would never take to the air in those conditions. And though we may enjoy reading his exploits and his flowery language, we are also no Saint-Exupéry. Still, these stories ask us to ponder the outlines of our own limits, point to where bravery and skill convene and act. For me, they shine a light on what I am willing to fly in and what I am not. I am not willing to fly the Hump, sure, but yesterday I was willing to soar over the (not as mighty but still intimidating) Sierra Nevada, and now I am headed to Death Valley, a place with a name both terrifying and apt.

...

The gyro skimmed desert landscape. I picked my way between rising cetacean peaks. I mostly followed a road, but sometimes the surface below was empty of anything man-made at all. When yet another 8,000-foot range loomed, I ascended once more, cresting crags that waved skyward and rocks that tilted at moonscape angles. It was both spooky and beautiful. When the flatlands beyond came finally into view, I caught my breath. Spread out before me was a blank beige canvas—Death Valley. But I was puzzled. There should be a tiny airstrip named Stovepipe Wells in front of me, over which I would turn south, heading to Furnace Creek, my stopover for the night. Instead, I saw nothing but one long scratch—an empty road that unfurled toward yet another set of peaks. I decided to start my descent anyway. I didn't want to be fixated on my map or anything inside the cockpit for too long; I wanted to set my course and then keep my gaze outward in order not to miss a thing, to stay fully present, to catch every detail. But . . . something wasn't right. I checked the purple GPS line shimmering on my tablet. In that moment I felt a tiny shift in my chest. My eyes ricocheted from map to tableau before me. I throttled way back, my mind insisting this was Death Valley, so start losing altitude. But there was no runway. And where was the low rock peninsula I should see to my right? I was lost, it seemed. But how could I be lost? I had two GPS maps open and one dormant, as well as a paper sectional somewhere at my feet (so terrible is my sense of direction that I carry backups to backups). I was mostly employing the final navigation technique, after dead reckoning and pilotage:

GPS. I was following a reliable line beamed to me by satellites. But why wasn't the ground matching my expectations?

This disorientation lasted only a few moments. I blame the way I was blindly following a line. I blame the way I had foolishly zoomed out my map, losing the exact topography. But I also blame the mammoth scale of the mountains I had been crossing, the weirdness of the landscape. I blame the dappling and stippling that made the rock seem to shape-shift as I passed over. I blame my natural intimidation of the *emptiness*, a landscape devoid of anything human except one paved road that had lost its cars many miles behind me and that now cut through the vista like a silent scar. I blame my realization that this was a part of the world that clearly wanted to kill me if I landed in it, with no visible water or shade. I blame my own neural system, scrambled by constant wind and pummeled by engine roar. I blame my open-mouthed awe. I felt lost, but I couldn't be lost. I was lost in my mind, at most. I laid two fingers on the tablet and widened the view.

There it was. By resorting to good old pilotage, I had reoriented myself. Comparing the map with the landscape now, I saw that there was in fact a smaller, higher valley before Death Valley. The sharpened topography on my tablet chastised: I still had more miles until the Stovepipe airstrip. I circled, catching my breath, shaking off the disorientation, trying not to excoriate myself. Looming above me like a huge staircase was another line of mountains to cross.

The crease I had descended into was called the Panamint Valley, according to the sectional on my lap. As I did slow circles to gain altitude, I gazed upward at the rock face that guarded it, called the Panamint Range. It reached to 11,000 feet and seemed to cast a shadow over me, it was so huge.

It's hard to describe how tiny I felt, how insignificant my emotions were, in that moment. I saw myself as if from afar, against the silent immovable stone, just a spinning yellow speck of . . . *what was that*, someone might say, *dust?* And it was how the moment stretched out behind me for a million years, and forward for another million, and here this rock was and would continue to be, while I would exist and then be swatted from that existence in a relative millisecond (like *that*, I imagined the cosmos saying, snapping its fingers to demonstrate just how quickly). Despite, or maybe because of, my unmoored self, any fear I felt eased into a deep wonder. I took slow breaths. My gyro swayed and swung and dipped in the turbulence. Still I rose. I was agog at the pilots of yore, who had terribly inaccurate paper maps, if any at all. As I crested the range, the full pageantry of the place took hold and I swiveled my head around, desperate to capture it. I exhaled and murmured *Wow, wowee* in rapid-fire succession. I wished suddenly that another human was here so I could point and gasp and they could point and gasp and my place in the universe would be secured. I declared out loud to no one that the Panamints were my new favorite place, their mind-boggling size and majesty the reason for what had happened, this directional lapse, this out-of-body hijacking. I continued, my engine the only sound for miles around. *Here I am*, I was calling to the world, *here I am*.

21

Groundspeed

By 1929, 9,500 Americans had a pilot's license (117 of them were women). Meanwhile, enthusiasts continued to innovate—planes became faster and more reliable. Inevitably, this trajectory had to be put on display. Inspired no doubt by that first air race, more cross-country dashes were organized, as well as compact short courses: slaloms flown at high speed and low altitude within view of crowds who thrilled at the planes zipping around grounded pylons at an altitude of 50 feet.

These air races were key to America's acceptance of flight. The pilots became the Instagram influencers of the day, but instead of fandom online with likes and comments, twenty-five thousand people might arrive in person to swarm a pilot who had landed at an airport to refuel, while six hundred thousand would gather at the final destination to greet the winning airplane or attend an air show. Air races were flamboyant affairs, and pilots who competed in them attracted sponsorship, recognition, and prize money.

No wonder women pilots, including Amelia Earhart, began agitating to race. They were met with the usual insistence that the flying skill and stamina needed, especially for the long-distance events, were impossible for women. Not to mention that unmentionable, *menstruation*. But then mentioned it was, and it was an absurdity: the aeronautics branch of the government advised, *"All women should be cautioned that it is dangerous for them to fly within a period extending from three days before, to three days after, the menstrual period."* Certainly head-to-head flights with men would be a disaster, they declared, offering instead a women-only race, but with a man in the cockpit. The women pilots refused. There was an ensuing brouhaha; ultimately, air race coordinators reluctantly organized the National Women's Air Derby, quickly dubbed the Powder Puff Derby by the press. It would not mandate a male copilot, but the women were relegated to flying only against one another. The course would resemble one flown by men, Santa Monica to Cleveland, but with more stops and a sleepover at night, much to the women's disgust. It was the best they would get, however, so the race proceeded.

Keith O'Brien's *Fly Girls: How Five Daring Women Defied All Odds and Made Aviation History* recounts how Derby planes were sabotaged at various stops, with tactics ranging from dirty gasoline to sawed brace wires to contaminated oil. When one pilot returned to her plane to check on it, she found every switch turned on. Race organizers insisted nothing was happening, but the women began to take turns keeping watch over their planes during stopovers, further abrading nerves through lack of sleep.

There were also the usual mishaps: Some pilots got lost, others were sidelined by mechanical failures. Bad weather hampered many. One mechanic flicked cigarette ash into a luggage compartment that ignited into a midflight fire. There were difficult landings. There was one fatal (and suspicious) crash; Marvel Crosson, who held an altitude record, among other firsts, was found dead in her wrecked Travel Air along a river. But compared to, say, a New York to Los Angeles race in which nine men had departed but only one had finished, it would be impossible to argue that the women weren't doing well (nineteen pilots entered, fifteen completed the race). After all, these were not novice pilots. Ruth Elder had attempted a transatlantic flight but had to ditch in the ocean. The long-distance aviator Evelyn Trout was known for flying expertly at night. Florence "Pancho" Barnes would eventually reach 191.19 miles per hour to break Earhart's speed record. But the denigration by press and organizers was constant. "Women are lacking in certain qualities that men possess." "Such races should be confined to men." In the end, Louise Thaden took the trophy, with Gladys O'Donnell second and Earhart coming in third.

Considering the bias and pressures, it was a wonder that by 1934, 625 American women had their pilot's license.

The low-altitude slalom air races of the early 1930s were dominated by the Gee Bee, a gallant plane with a stubby profile, a mono wing, and a top speed of 150 miles per hour. But problems developed—famous (male) pilots would lose control of the aircraft and auger into the ground; in one instance a wing was seen to break away during a speed record attempt. The aviator Jimmy Doolittle, who would go on to become famous for the World War II bombing campaign against Japan called the Doolittle Raid, exclaimed that "to fly that plane is exactly like the task of balancing an ice cream cone on the top of one's finger."

By 1933, Florence Klingensmith was considered one of the best race pilots in the country, practically smothered in that go-grease, everyone agreed. Yet when she was killed in the Gee Bee during the first race ever against men, lack of skill was cited as the cause. This despite the crowds watching as she made a blazing turn ("Just look at the girl make that perfect bank!" shouted the announcer with glee). But their admiration turned to horror as the wing began to separate. Klingensmith steered away from the crowd to spare lives and then tried to gain altitude for a parachute jump. Instead, pilot and plane plummeted to the ground.

Investigators ultimately admitted that the wing had failed, but public opinion ignored this fact. One witness interviewed for the inquest felt free to speculate, "I believe she possibly fainted and leaned forward into that there stick, throwing the plane into a dangerous dive." Immediately, women were banned from air races altogether. Yet the men kept dying (a third of all the male-only cross-country Bendix racers crashed during its five years—half never finished). A year after Klingensmith's Gee Bee accident, the famed aviator Douglas Davis nose-dived his own Gee Bee during a race, killing himself. But his skill never came into question. Instead, it was quickly decided that the Gee Bee "was an experimental plane, flying at a fast speed, on a bumpy day. There's no doubt something gave way. There's nothing further to investigate." Turns out, his aircraft's wing had sheared off too. Finally, slowly, Klingensmith's death was reframed.

Aviators like Amelia Earhart clamored for inclusion back into men's races, and it was finally agreed that the cross-country 1936 Bendix race would allow women to race against the men. It was thought that each female pilot would pair with a man, but Louise

Thaden and Blanche Noyes—who later so successfully picked barns on which to "air mark" town names for navigation—entered as a team. This move was met with the usual dismay and doubt, even though both women were veterans of cross-country flights and record-setting aviators.

Thaden and Noyes won the race.

Two years later, the beautician mogul turned aviator Jacqueline Cochran also beat the male field. Cochran would go on to become the first person to fly over 20,000 feet, and during World War II she organized and commanded the Women Airforce Service Pilots (WASPs). These were civilian women with private pilot certifications assigned noncombat tasks, freeing up men to fight overseas.

The WASPs were not the only American women involved in the war—more than 350,000 served in various capacities. But as Molly Merryman, who wrote *Clipped Wings: The Rise and Fall of the Women Airforce Service Pilots of World War II*, points out, the WASPs differed because these women were not plunked into traditional roles, such as secretaries and nurses. Instead, they were working pilots who "served in positions desired and admired by men . . . in the proving ground of masculinity." This inadvertently challenged what the culture believed was possible and suitable for women at the time.

The WASPs ferried aircraft, piloted male navigators, bombardiers, and gunners during training, and towed strafing targets. They also came in handy when male pilots balked at planes they deemed unsafe, like the B-26 Marauder, nicknamed the Murderer. Commanders would shame the hesitant men by assigning WASPs to fly the unruly aircraft instead, leading to publicity like the article titled "Sugar and Spice! B-26 as Gentle as a Lamb in the Hands of WASPs," which enthused that "the announcement of young women flying the Marauder is the second piece of overwhelming evidence that proves the Martin bomber is NOT a tough plane to fly."

Statistics show that the WASPs were on par with or better than male pilots flying similar domestic duties when it came to errors (a 0.001 percentage vs. a 0.006 percentage) and accident rates (0.060 per 1,000 hours vs. 0.062 per 1,000 hours), with less sick time (surely the military thought women would be regularly felled by menstruation, but no).

There were requirements to become a WASP. Formally, you had to be over five feet four inches tall, between the ages of twenty-one and thirty-five, and have thirty-five hours of flying time. Informally, the WASPs were almost exclusively white. Only two Asian Americans, one Native American, and two Mexican Americans served, and all Black Americans were turned away, including Janet Bragg, the first Black woman in the country to earn a full commercial pilot's license (she would later establish her own airport), as well as Mildred Hemmons Carter, who flew as a Tuskegee Airman in their Civilian Pilot Training Program.

Officially, women were still barred from the armed forces, so not only did their heroism and service go unrecognized for decades, but the lifelong medical and financial benefits given to male servicemembers were denied them (in addition, when a WASP died in the line of duty, fellow WASPs had to pass the hat to pay for the return of her body to her hometown). But their sacrifice prevailed. After a prolonged legal fight, WASPs were finally accorded veteran status, on November 23, 1977.

22

Airspeed

On our instrument panel is a tiny identifier called a *transponder*. On a normal day, air traffic control might ask that we dial in or "squawk" a specific number that differentiates us from other traffic on their radar as we approach. There also may be a request to "ident," or push a transponder button; this immediately highlights Woodstock on their busy screens. But the transponder has another use: dialing in the numbers 7700 means there's an onboard emergency of some sort; 7600 means radio communication has been lost. The numbers 7500? You are surreptitiously telling authorities that you've been hijacked.

Hijacking is not an aerial event that will affect me in flight; for one, the gyrocopter can carry only one passenger, so odds are good that mine is not a desperate criminal. Also, the gyro chugs along at a comparatively anemic 90 miles per hour or so and stays aloft for about three and a half hours before it needs refueling, making it the world's most unimpressive heist. Still, all pilots

Why Fly

have been assiduously schooled on how to alert the authorities of a cockpit takeover, using that magic transponder code, 7500.

When the first American commercial plane was "skyjacked," as it was called then, there was no airport security, such as luggage checks or pat-downs, for fear customers would feel inconvenienced, even violated. Privacy was paramount as, it seems, was trust. It was 1961, and the ease with which weapons could be brought onto planes was laughable. The airlines' quick capitulation to a skyjacker's demands also made it a relatively uncomplicated caper, and by the early seventies, skyjackings surged; sometimes two commercial flights were commandeered on the same day. My own godfather recalled being a passenger on a hijacked plane, and he claimed it didn't even feel scary, so routine was the event.

It was more than just the ease of the crime that lured its perpetrators: there was something about the power and romance of the airplane that beckoned. "It is no accident that the epidemic began to crest as the last vestiges of 1960s idealism were being extinguished," says Brendan Koerner in his book on plane hijackings, *The Skies Belong to Us*, pointing out that "there was no more spectacular way for the marginalized to feel the rush of power" than theatrically using a plane to take hostages, demand money, and fly to the destination of their choice. That destination was often Cuba, where, contrary to what the hijackers believed, Prime Minister Fidel Castro did not welcome them with open arms as compatriots; he would often arrest and imprison them. He would then gleefully impound the American plane, returning it for a fee. To deter these skyjackings, the U.S. State Department lit on an idea that for some inexplicable reason seemed to make more sense than simply tightening up airport security: it decided to offer free one-way flights to Cuba to anyone who agreed never to return.

In the end the idea was scrapped when Castro refused to let these planes land at all.

Angsty teenagers, a coal miner with black lung who wanted a free flight to Israel to work on a kibbutz before dying, a veteran mad at the IRS, a former New York City police officer who asked for half a million dollars, a young girl who strapped road flares around her body and stated that her mother's boyfriend (imprisoned for skyjacking) must be freed. These were some of the bumbling, attention-seeking, mentally ill, or just plain desperate people behind the aerial crimes. One skyjacker tried to exit midflight with his ransom haul but was foiled by the crew when he had to put down his weapon to fiddle with his newly purchased parachute equipment. Eleven days later, a man wearing sunglasses and carrying a ticket bearing the name Dan Cooper and a suitcase that he claimed contained a bomb commandeered a Northwest Orient airplane. He demanded and received $200,000 and four parachutes, one of which he donned over the Pacific Northwest. He jumped from the open aft door and, since a body was never found, quickly became the mythic figure we now call D.B. Cooper, whose whereabouts and identity are unknown to this day.

The initial skyjackings were nonviolent, but hijackers were later in danger of being unceremoniously offed by fed-up pilots carrying their own gun in the cockpit. In 1971 the first passenger death occurred, and the airlines realized that their fear of losing customers through increased security measures was now trumped by the increasing danger of a violent air incident. The year 1972 saw forty skyjackers making demands in U.S. skies. Security was finally tightened in 1973 and skyjackings dropped, with a brief exception in the early eighties, when twenty-five planes were hijacked, almost all to Havana by immigrant Cubans who wanted to return home.

The events of September 11, 2001, when terrorists commandeered and ultimately crashed three planes, signaled a tragic resurgence. On that day, 2,977 people died and thousands more were injured, and with that came the end of any deference to inconvenience, any waffling about security. Now it's belts off, arms up for the pat-downs, reinspection of bags, throw away water and shampoo, are these deer antlers okay (yes), are these darts okay (no). Gone are the days of the easy airline rustle. Vigilance is too high for the rapscallion or the rogue or the simply addled to poach an airplane. Skyjackings have faded from view.

. . .

Mathias Rust was nineteen when in 1987 he used a small single engine airplane and his mere twenty-five hours (post-certification) of flight experience to make a grand gesture of a different sort: his own declaration of peace between the West and the Soviet Union during a time of high tension and failed diplomatic talks. Why Rust thought he should be that messenger is unclear, but at the time I too was young and idealistic, as well as a pilot, so I read about his exploit with fascination.

Rust left his home in West Germany and flew a circuitous route over two weeks, building up his confidence and his flying hours and making pit stops in places like Iceland and the Faroe Islands. Ultimately, he backtracked to Helsinki, telling air traffic control that he was heading to Sweden. Instead, he flew over Estonia and eventually to Red Square in Moscow. There he swooped down to 30 feet but decided against landing because of the crowds and the risk of hurting someone. He made a few passes, eventually touching down on a nearby bridge. Curious Russians swarmed him for an hour before he was arrested.

Among Rust's possessions was a manifesto that he planned to hand to the Russian leader, Mikhail Gorbachev. This is the playbook of many crackpots, and indeed there were many who saw his whole plan as lunacy. But this is also the playbook of youth: a wildly ambitious and flamboyant act, along with an improbable vision set down (at length) on paper. Rust later told *Smithsonian* magazine in 2005 that he reasoned that if he made it to Moscow, "how could Reagan continue to say it was an 'Empire of Evil' if me, in a small aircraft, can go straight there and be unharmed?"

Rust was unharmed, but not from any charity on the part of the Soviet Union. He had been met with almost comedic mismanagement and a large dose of luck: the Air Defense Forces had been recently reorganized and there remained confusion between sectors; Rust's plane was seen on radar but mistaken for migrating geese, even though by flying eastward it was agreed the "geese" were migrating in the wrong direction; a downed plane the day before meant that civilian aircraft aiding in the search were flying in unlikely places anyway. He had been approached midflight multiple times by fighter jets but never shot down, though it is not clear why. This despite the West German flag decal displayed on the aircraft's tail. Perhaps it was just too improbable an enemy—a small Cessna 172, poking along in hostile airspace, making no effort to evade radar. To top off this string of absurdity and good fortune, the bridge Rust eventually picked as his landing spot was usually striped with trolley wires. These had been removed just that morning, with plans to reinstall them a day later.

Ironically, Rust's grand gesture did facilitate peace. But not in the way he had expected. Neither the "imaginary bridge" of his flight from West to East nor his heady manifesto had an impact. Instead, Gorbachev used Rust's entry into Russian airspace and the ensuing pratfalls as a reason to fire many of the air defense officers standing in the way of his plans for economic reform and political liberalization. Hundreds of opponents were removed under the pretext that they had embarrassed and endangered the country. Gorbachev signed an arms reduction agreement with Ronald Reagan soon after.

Rust himself was charged with entering Russia illegally, flouting airspace regulations, and general "hooliganism" (an actual legal term). He denied only the last charge, saying he was promoting world peace, and how hooligan could that be? Rust was sentenced to four years in a labor camp but ended up being freed and deported within a year and a half.

It's unclear whether Rust knew he was following the footsteps of Nazi deputy führer Rudolf Hess, who himself claimed to be on a mission of peace when he stole a Messerschmitt from a Munich base on the evening of May 10, 1941, and flew it on a perilous journey across the North Sea to Scotland. He navigated in pitch dark, fog, and in danger of being shot down by the British defense forces. Once in Scotland, he ran out of fuel. He abandoned his plane by parachute over a dark field, just short of his destination.

His plan was to reach a specific landowner in Scotland who he believed (mistakenly) to be part of an underground British cabal sympathetic to Hitler and therefore willing to encourage their prime minister, Winston Churchill, to negotiate with the Nazi leader. Hess later told the interrogators who arrested him that he saw himself as the liaison between Britain and Hitler, brokering a deal in which Britain would agree to stand down from defending Europe, and in return Hitler would refrain from invading England. The furtive flight, he said, was unsanctioned by the Reich; it was his own private war strategy.

Why would Hess—a top-ranking Nazi—undertake such a dangerous excursion, land in enemy territory, and think he could execute such a loony plan? His reasoning remains murky. Did Hitler secretly send him? Did he believe the war was doomed and only a treaty could save his beloved Reich? Did covert British operatives somehow persuade him to undertake the plan? Or, with his position in the Reich becoming precarious, did he simply hope to impress the Führer by setting up a negotiation? Whatever his motivation, he made the flight against the backdrop of what seems to have been a slipping mental state (and possibly methamphetamines, since most of the Reich leaders consistently overindulged in drugs, mostly stimulants). Indeed, Hess showed paranoia and instability until his death at the age of ninety-three by apparent suicide, still imprisoned.

Mathias Rust has also led a checkered and violent afterlife. Just a few years after being freed in Russia, he stabbed a woman who rejected his advances. He was later arrested for shoplifting and tax fraud. He has dabbled in cults. Most recently he claimed to be a yoga teacher and a financial adviser, as well as to be completely reformed, blaming his former life of crime on trauma from his Soviet imprisonment so many years ago.

These days, grand gestures by plane are limited. They might include a little bragging at a bar about one's flying escapades. A splurge on the latest avionics to impress pals. Or, if you aren't a pilot, you enlist one to write a marriage proposal across the sky, resplendent letters that shine, then bloat, then slowly fade away.

23

Pilot Error

I recently received an email from someone I didn't know. It was two sentences long. *Hmmmmm . . . expired Class 3, No Basic Med, NTSB report, deregistered aircraft. Please don't include yourself in our aviation community.*

To say I was taken aback is to put it mildly. This was a labor-intensive note: some stranger took the time to go into my FAA files. Some stranger took the time to find my email address. Some stranger took the time to write and send a note that purposely began with that contemptuous drawn-out *Hmmmmm* and went on from there. There was such animosity. There was no curiosity.

Too bad he (it was a he, which will not surprise all the shes who fly) didn't check with me first on the context of the facts.

My third class medical certificate is expired because I have not flown under private pilot rules for years. Nor do I need a Basic Med (also a health certification); I fly under a different ticket called "sport pilot," and what is required for that is a valid

Why Fly

driver's license and the presumed medical health that goes with it. I have deregistered an aircraft, required because I sold it to a buyer in Argentina.

So this person was the one who didn't fully understand regulations, seemed remiss in the aviation community. Yet the email still felt cruel and unnecessary, and I wondered at the anger behind it.

The stranger was right on one point: I have had an accident, for which I dutifully filed an NTSB report. It remains the most humiliating event of my long years and hovers on the top of my list of life regrets. So when this man with way too much time on his hands added that he would like me to remove myself from the aviation community (*his* aviation community), I sort of understood why.

A mistake in Silicon Valley is greeted with fanfare. A mistake in relationships is considered a learning experience. But in aviation, a community that has spent decades convincing outsiders how safe its passion is, an accident among the tribe is a disappointment. And I agree. When this man spits out this two-sentence missive, I concede that there is something there.

An accident is the pinnacle of stupidity, mostly because it is usually the culmination of small, avoidable mistakes, as mine was, resulting in one momentous occasion, which we sum up as "pilot error." Pilot error is responsible for almost every predicament an aviator encounters. Sudden fog bank? You didn't check the weather. Engine out? Your preflight was incomplete or your maintenance was lacking.

To this day I go over the chain of mishaps and denials that led to my own pilot error like a trichotillomaniac examining every split end before pulling the hair out. At every one of those intersections, a different decision would have averted what eventually became a plummet to earth.

On that fateful day, it was windy. Very windy. I stood in the hangar with my friend and fellow trike pilot Jim and my new girlfriend. She had never been to a small airport or inside a hangar or flown in a trike before. For all these reasons, against a backdrop of deep infatuation, I flung myself into the land of pilot error.

First, I ignored important details about the aircraft I was flying, most notably that I was having trouble with it. Specifically, my new wing was squirrelly and petulant in anything but calm air, becoming more so whenever I hit turbulence or thermals. I had flown a wing this size before with no issues. I guessed instead that one wingtip was out of whack, somehow not in accordance with factory specs, needed to be tuned. But fixing an experimental craft is always difficult. A trike is a strange satyr of hang glider above and motored craft below; it was hard to find reliable advice. Expert hang glider pilots could assess the wing but couldn't fly the trike, and seasoned mechanics wouldn't understand hang glider wings. No one I knew could figure out what was going on or had any insight on who might. The problem remained unfixed. Of course I could have dismantled the wing, boxed it, and sent it back to the factory asking that it be tested. That is what I *should* have done. But such a time-consuming and technical task was daunting. I took the easier route: before each flight I embarked on a simple calculus of my own skills and the wing's hissy-fits and invariably concluded that since nothing had gone terribly wrong so far, nothing would go terribly wrong now. This is called *normalcy bias* in social science terms, but most of us recognize it for what it is: magical thinking.

Second, I decided to believe that the burly wind conditions beginning to shake the hangar doors and whirl the windsock around were not really that bad, and anyway, they would lessen as the evening approached and the temperatures dropped. This too is so common in humans that it has its own scientific term: *optimism bias*.

Let's be clear: When Jim said *Let's fly*, I hesitated. But I didn't say no. I looked at the trike, the wind, and the eager face of my current crush (and, as it turned out, future wife), and I said *Sure*, with a nonchalant shrug. The social science term for this common affliction is called *wanting to impress*. Of course, I wouldn't fly passengers with my wing undiagnosed and problematic (this is called *a glimmer of common sense*), but Jim was happy to squire a beautiful young woman around the sky in his own perfectly working trike (Note: this beautiful young woman had a fear of flying but seemed eager to hop into the open cockpit aircraft anyway; she too was also apparently afflicted with some sort of impress-her-itis.)

Once in the air it was clear to me that the turbulence was too much for my wing. I tried different altitudes to no avail. Meanwhile, in Jim's trike, my beloved was reportedly gleeful. They headed for the coast and views of hills and ocean. After getting thrown around for a while, I radioed I was returning to the airport. A few minutes later, Jim, also experiencing uncomfortable turbulence, decided to turn around too.

I tuned in to the automated weather station for updated wind speeds, gusts, and direction, and what I heard did not make me happy. The conditions had worsened dramatically. Gusts were higher than I'd ever flown in. They were hitting the runway from unappealing angles. But why did I even bother with the numbers? I knew the shitshow by the way I was gripping the bar as if it was a cliff I dangled from. I couldn't even key the mic because my thumb kept bouncing off the button. Being knocked around was not a new feeling. I was used to a low "wing loading," in which the wingspan is large and the corresponding weight of the craft is light. This makes trike pilots much like migrating monarch butterflies shot-putted by the jet stream. We are corks on a rolling sea. Cessna and Piper pilots at the hold short line liked to peer at us on approach out of their sturdy enough cockpits, aghast at the way we shimmied and twerked in the sky. So, knocked around, no big deal. But knocked around and out of control was a feeling I did not like. I was sweating. I was gritting my teeth. I was muttering half sentences to myself. Below, the windsock jerked and swung.

Honestly, I still could have landed safely. A string of stupid errors had put me here, but I was a skilled trike pilot and an experienced aviator. There remained good decisions to make.

But on the downwind leg, with hearth and home so close, get-on-the-ground-itis begin to bloom inside me. This urgency to land *now, now, now* was understandable, yet that was exactly the time I should have refocused, shed attachment, dismissed quickly this dysfunctional need to touch wheels onto solid asphalt. I should have thought, *Hey, this feels wrong, I'm stepping away from this plan*. In my daily life, I would have noticed the red flag that is the push to *hurry, hurry, make that decision*. I would have stopped, frowned, reassessed. The truth is that I hate hurrying. And if someone tries to rush me to a choice, I back away. In short, I should have backed away. The aviation equivalent of this is the *go-around*.

The go-around is the aborting of a landing that is threatening to go awry. Go-arounds are an essential physical skill, but they also require an equally essential emotional aptitude.

Why Fly

You must hold two things at once—the image of the softest of landings, and yet also the abort, pushing the throttle forward to leap back into the sky. A pilot in trouble is often afflicted so badly with get-on-the-ground-itis that she sees only one option, and it pulses and shines and calls like the ancient song of the sirens.

Come here. Come down. Escape this maelstrom.

I turned onto the final leg and the runway unfurled before me. There was still time to realize that a go-around offered the best hope: circling the traffic pattern might allow my head to clear, let me fully assess the turbulence brawling on the lee side of the hangars, maybe even bring a positive change in wind gusts. Instead I crimped my shoulders, set my jaw, let get-on-the-ground-itis fully engulf me, and attempted to land.

The centerline flung itself about. The trike jumped and dropped and tilted. I pulled the bar in close, eyes glued to the ground, my brain yelling to go *fast, fast, fast* to avoid the dreaded stall. At various points on this trajectory I should have powered my way out and tried again. Instead, what happened next is a little murky. I may have been punched by a downdraft. Or the tweaked wingtip stalled. All I know is that at a certain height above the runway the trike dropped.

It's uninteresting from here. I lived. I shattered one ankle, sprained my arm, cut open my head. Jim landed without mishap, and within moments my infatuation was running toward me like in the movies, arms outspread, crying, throwing her arms around me. But it wasn't the movies, this was real life, and all I felt was deep, deep shame. Jim arrived next. He picked his way across the downed wing and canted fuselage and knelt next to me and I whispered to him, *I feel so humiliated*, and he said, *I understand, sweetheart*, and held my hand.

Pilot Error

This was decades ago. As the years passed, and my wife recalled the event, she often stuck on this exchange. Humiliation? *That* was my primary reaction? Not fear, not pain, not relief at being alive? When other people were around, she spoke with jest and feigned disbelief. But when she talked to me alone it was with confusion. She couldn't understand it at all. To her a crash is a random act of God, an aberrant flick from the fingers of an uncaring universe. I've tried to explain how the event was human-tarnished through and through, pilot error that stretched back days, weeks, months, from beginning to sad, definitive end. *It's just a mistake*, she would counter, as if mistakes are bestowed on you like falling rain and easily shaken off, and are not instead that determined march through forks in the road in which you repeatedly pick the wrong fork and refuse to turn around.

I think: Traditionally when we tell our lover we are leaving for good, we say earnestly, "It's me, not you." But do we really mean it? *It's totally you*, we are thinking inside. I am here to tell you: In a pilot's relationship to her aircraft, "It's me, not you," pretty much always holds true. Pilot error is responsible for almost every bad outcome, if not every single one.

. . .

If you're a pilot, you no doubt have many opinions, assessments, evaluations of this whole chain of events. I appreciate that. But there's nothing you can add that I have not already thought of, felt, flogged myself with, reexperienced. No letters please. Certainly you have your own misadventures with pilot error and if you were lucky they went unnoticed, there were no catastrophic consequences, and you clocked each instance as something you will never do again. The door that flies open on takeoff but is quickly closed, the weather that descends on you but you narrowly skirt, the leaking hose/broken wire/loose screw you did not catch on preflight, or that cat I mentioned earlier that you failed to find napping inside your wing and that emerges just after takeoff, fur blowing in the wind, paws locked over a strut, trying to decide whether to leap onto your head. You chastise yourself, breathe deeply, make a mental note, and never have to file a report. I wish that version of pilot error for each and every one of you.

There was an unintended bright side to this catastrophe, however. Without this accident, I might never have had my wonderful marriage. That is the irony: This relationship, the one I now mourn through flight, was also cemented through flight (and loss of flight). At the time of this skirmish I so decisively lost, we had been together only six months. And yet she stayed. She took assiduous care of me. She swabbed my leaky wounds, my tremulous heart. She inspected the catheter, plumped the pillows, meted out the meds. Meanwhile I was a certifiable mess: I wept all the time, hobbled around on crutches. I was fragile, she nursed; it's fair to say that we were shocked by our respective weaknesses and strengths, these sides of ourselves that rose to the occasion. Long after I healed, we continued to do this so well: coax open the other's best self. We became good partners, and remained so for many years. And then a different kind of crash, in slow motion, over time, aviators in air that became turbulent, so that our wingtips, faulty, out of tune, repeatedly uncared for, finally betrayed.

PART 7

LANDING

Now he knew what Shalimar knew: If you surrendered to the air, you could ride it.

TONI MORRISON, *SONG OF SOLOMON*

24

Traffic Pattern

"A landing," muses the author Mark Vanhoenacker, "is nothing less than how we move from the skies of our planet to its surface. It's how we (a flying species at last) come home."

He is speaking about home in the most existential sense. That place we are threaded into. That simple emotional brocade, made less of mass and more of time; those moments that resonate with warmth and acceptance. But Vanhoenacker also means home at its most quotidian: whence we came, that clapboard outline inside which we go about our day. It is, put plain and simple, our sweet planet, hung delicately in vast dark space and, for the incoming pilot at least, our runway, that tiny, recognizable stripe of gray that awaits.

From above, Earth is a batik. It is all swirl and color. It is beautiful, but also distant, a symbol of hearth but not an actual hearth. From 3,000 feet, say, Earth appears inert, just a metonym for all the things we love and cherish. But descend toward the textures, and then the indifferent clod comes alive with moving cars and trees that sway and kids on playing fields who converge and scatter and converge again like fretful clouds. We drop from the finicky grasp of a capacious sky toward the familiar and warm. (I mean that literally as well as figuratively. The air is usually warmer closer to the ground, cooling upward by an average 3.5 degrees Fahrenheit for every thousand feet. I say "usually" because there may be an inversion layer, where the temperature is actually higher at a greater altitude. The sky is full of uncertainty.) It's easy to be charmed by landings, that beckoning tarmac in sight, that growing welcome of familiar shapes, the genuflection of the sky that is really the lowering of the aircraft itself.

Landing is also where all the forces of lift, weight, drag, and thrust become most tangible, take shape in all your senses. There is the sight of the numbers growing bigger in the windshield as gravity begins its new winning streak. There is the kinetic feel of the heavier foot pressure on the left rudder to counter propeller torque. There is the sound of the engine eased back to lose altitude.

But we know that being close to the ground, as comforting as it may feel, is a dangerous place for a pilot. There is less room for recovery from errors, diminishing second chances. And landing is the most technically difficult part of flying (but not the most dangerous—that belongs to the takeoff, as noted before). It is that phase of flight that most completely calls upon the skills needed to fly a plane, from speed control, to radio savvy, to stall avoidance, to balanced turns, to head-on-a-swivel, to adjusting for wind direction, to risk assessment, to separation from other aircraft and more. To top it off, landing requires all those skills *and* a higher level of finesse when employing them. For this reason I practice landings constantly—as many as, say, seven in one flight. Round and round my airport runway I go, like a carousel. In this way I slough off the reflexes for walking or driving a car or typing on a computer. I reset them for the loose grip on the stick, the light pressure on the throttle. If I'm landing smoothly, I may leave for the ocean, the hills, that other airport, early; if not, it's the call that I am *on the go*, that once more I am *closed traffic*. I simulate an engine-out here, I perform a vertical descent touchdown there.

Landings are also difficult because they occur in the busiest part of the sky—over the airfield. At larger airports, air traffic controllers order us about like schoolteachers on a playground, blowing proverbial whistles to get our attention, vectoring us into a cross-the-street line so no one is hurt or lost. At smaller airports there are no controllers; instead, it is up to incoming pilots to work together, and to help with that we have a specific radio channel for each airport. We approach like polite strangers ready with small talk. We announce ourselves and then carefully join a prescribed queue called the *traffic pattern*, that invisible boxlike roadway that all pilots agree on to manage this unusually crowded area of sky. Here we become the best version of ourselves: humans cooperating. We send salutations of our impending arrival from miles out, then reintroduce ourselves at preset points. These invisible points hover at certain altitudes and angles to the runway, so that each pilot knows exactly where to look for the small mote of you against the tumbles of green and blue and brown and white. It's surprisingly difficult to spot an incoming aircraft, especially during the day; at night one's strobing navigation lights will help, though a starry sky or a brightly lit city can confuse. Even the recommended scanning technique we learn is far from fail-safe, moving the eyes horizontally and halting every few degrees for two seconds, a sort of eyeball shiver: shift, stop, shift, stop. Add to that the checklist that demands attention to configure the faster, fancier aircraft for landing, and the avionics tsking silent reprimands—airspeed! rpms! everything in the green! The result is many distractions at a time when keen attention is paramount. And so we turn in our invisible rectangle, keying our mics at intervals, this waving of our hands to say *We are here, and now we are here,* a strange and comforting bonhomie. Meanwhile we are also marking ourselves for those on the ground, who shudder and whirr through their final run-up or wait at the hold short line—we don't want them pulling out onto the runway as we descend toward them.

All this is done even if there is no one else around, because who knows? Someone might appear. Someone might even be there, with no modern avionics that make them at least a blip on my screen, and they might be thinking that no one else is there too. But often someone else *is* there. She is fluttering ahead or coming in behind, also calling out her position, and we sound back and forth, like whales across an ocean.

Traffic pattern language is intentionally stripped of color. The goal is friendly but not chatty, blunt but not terse. There is little emotion. I tend to err toward a monotone, a bad habit from my years as a firefighter, when it was imperative to keep your voice as nonchalant as possible even as the house was collapsing in flames around you. What is called "interrupting" in a conversation on the ground is called "stepping on" up here, and unlike conversations on the ground, being stepped on in the air blocks one's transmission entirely, and this can be dangerous because (also unlike conversations on the ground) each transmission is vital. We speak quickly but clearly, in a language that uses no adjectives and few articles, just verbs and nouns sung with great efficiency, like infants. *Pleasantville traffic, experimental gyro, turning base* is the pilot version of Me, Hungry, Down.

The traffic pattern is a line dance, a meditation labyrinth, a grocery store line, our pagan religion. It is that tacit agreement keeping chaos and collision and general savagery at bay as we return, finally, home. Yet there are pilots who disregard its sanctity and these rituals. They may figure that the airport is so sleepy, why does it matter? They opt to barge in on the base leg, or fly a final "straight in" from ten miles out, which is the aviation equivalent of cutting to the front of the line and then having a long argument with the bouncer about your ID while others wait behind. "Straight in" is pilotspeak for one long lumber on an extended trajectory toward the airport. It means the rest of us in the pattern must constantly worry about the incoming plane. *Should I extend my downwind, is it safe for me to be on final, can I roll onto the runway*, all questions and calculations a pilot shouldn't have to make, that the traffic pattern is there to automatically solve, as long as everyone is in it, compliant. Unfortunately, "straight in" is not just rude, it can be fatal.

I was almost annihilated out of the sky one day when a pilot decided to fly straight in. There were three of us in the pattern dutifully calling our turns. I called my final and was poking along at the necessary height, speed, track of my gyrocopter. Meanwhile another gyro with an instructor and student waited at the hold short line on the ground. They were watching my glide path, maybe the instructor was even critiquing/dissecting/praising it for his student, and thank God for that, because suddenly, behind me and unbeknownst to me, a speeding low wing appeared. The instructor radioed *Airplane on final do you see the gyro ahead, do you see the gyro.* I misunderstood, thinking he was talking about an aircraft in the pattern that I had already calculated my separation from; I radioed back *No problem I'm almost down.* What I couldn't see (and shouldn't have had to see)

Why Fly

was that this was an entirely new interloper, big and fast and gaining quickly. The interloper finally made a call about being *on final*, but I still didn't grasp the danger I was in. I possess good situational awareness, gleaned from years of flight without fancy avionics, and had clocked who was (supposedly) in the pattern, that no one (supposedly) was close. I was on final, I had priority, my job now was to land; any plane behind was responsible for what we call "separation," which is a fancy way of saying not killing me.

The instructor yelled into his radio again, this time his voice tipping from urgent to frantic—*theresagyroonfinaltheresagyroonfinal*. Simultaneously, I must have suddenly come into the interloper's view, a small yellow rotorcraft now ballooning in his windshield. He banked at the last millisecond. Then he was on my right side, thundering by me. My heart almost seized, understanding in a flash what had just been averted.

How had this happened? Those of us in the pattern were calling every leg. There were three of us, so the chatter was consistent. The ceiling was low that day (but legal for us VFR pilots); the interloper had dropped out of the clouds. He was already close to the airport, already lined up for final, tuning in to our radio frequency late. Then he rocketed straight in. Was he in a hurry? Was he distracted by his transition from IFR to a visual landing? Was he just taking his chances, thinking that a small airport was a quiet airport? I will never know. What is certain is that for all his fancy avionics, he had forgotten basic flight skills, the ones that Saint-Exupéry, the mail pilot Beryl Markham, and every single Alaskan bush pilot stick to: keep situational awareness, repeatedly scan outside the cockpit, maintain head-on-a-swivel, think a few steps ahead. In an eerie coincidence, there had been an incident at a small airport just weeks before that matched this scenario to a T. Almost. That one had ended in collision, and death.

The traffic pattern, then, is the opposite of what we want in our grounded life. It is the aviation equivalent of scheduled sex. Predictable and healthy, it welcomes the mundane, cherishes limited conversation, banishes surprises. Here, same-old, same-old is the hope. Bland, whispered clichés are expected. Familiarity doesn't breed contempt. Accordingly, there are rarely misunderstandings; squabbles are almost nonexistent. There are just a few goals: take off and land safely, avoid collisions.

One day, while setting up to land, I heard a call over the radio for an emergency. The pilot didn't say "Mayday," but I could hear the tension in his voice. He was having trouble with his engine, said he was coming straight in. This situation was an appropriate use of straight in.

I was on downwind, and I just stayed the course, knowing I would extend the leg until the plane in question had landed. There was no other traffic circling. Soon the stricken plane came into view, a tiny crucifix against the sky. I didn't know what to say, so I offered what I could, which was the respect of a blank airwave, keeping the radio uncluttered for the pilot to concentrate on whatever chaos was happening in his cockpit. It felt like just him and me in the sky, and I watched and waited.

Suddenly another voice chimed in. "The landing checklist, it's easy to forget that. Get your gear down, flaps right. Like any other landing. You're going to be fine, buddy." The stricken pilot radioed back, his voice shaking and high, "Yeah, thank you, right."

Turns out there were others up here, listening, hoping.

The advice about the checklist and landing gear was needed, but those of us on the channel knew it was more than that. We heard it for what it was deeper down: an acknowledgment of how alone that pilot must feel in his metal fuselage and his predicament, and then a reaching out anyway, to say *Hey, we're here, we're rooting for you,* and more than that *We so understand, we have your back, and damn to hell this flip side of flying*—a finicky plane, an uncertain landing, our mortal tendency toward pilot error. My throat tightened. *Humanity*, I thought, and my eyes teared. Then I watched the little white fixed wing float in safely and land without mishap. "Thanks for the help, guys," the pilot said, relief streaming from his voice. Now we all keyed our mics, disembodied humans circling above, breaking radio protocol and chanting *Good job, good job, glad it worked out, go have a beer.*

I'll skip the minutiae of how to fly the traffic pattern; just know that as you enter this imaginary road that snakes in a particular way, you use the time to check wind conditions, glance at instruments, clock other aircraft in the pattern, gently lose altitude, and adjust to the right landing speed. It is much like the pat-down we do before any important meeting (this one with the earth) when we check teeth for spinach, peer close for makeup smears, do one small half turn in the mirror. As we approach the runway head-on (as noted above, this is called simply "final"), we abandon all this and concentrate mostly on lining up. I remind myself that an abort is always an option, I find my touchdown point. All instruments except maybe the airspeed indicator are abandoned and I become a bodily thing, a kinetic avionic. Wind shifts are felt through fingers and feet. My right and left hands—the former on the stick, the latter on the throttle—anticipate each other like mirror twins. My eyes center the white line in my windshield.

Finally the runway is beneath me. I lift the nose slightly (we call this the "flare"); landing is not a collision with the earth, it is more a skimming, slowing, settling. Here is the final negotiation between lift and gravity, when lift slowly leaves the building with a regal wave. There is always that last act of resistance, though, the recalcitrant float caused by a compressed downwash of our own making, called *ground effect*. Sometimes, if I've come in too fast or twitched the stick with the wrong amount of finesse or a gust has hit or any number of minute issues, the ground effect balloons me up again. No need for panic, just an adjustment of the pitch so that finally the main wheels touch softly, like a sigh, and then the nose wheel follows, and the whole gyro slows, slows, slows. Then I accelerate again, take off, practice one more time.

Surely the households that ring the airfield hate me and my buzzing yellow bug, but they never call to complain because I'm obeying the rules, these rules for airports, not suburbs. I imagine the residents stewing and ruing below me, shaking fists at the heavens. Honestly, I don't like to upset people, but there was no mistaking their home's location when they moved in. Still the houses crawl inward. I often wonder how the developers unload these huge mansions built so decisively under an unruly sky. Perhaps real estate agents show the houses only in unflyable weather. Or they feed syrupy, bald-faced lies: *Caught it on a busy day! There are rumors it will close soon. Everyone says they get used to it.* Because why would anyone with means say yes to the ridiculously fancy abode I can see on the downwind leg, with the pool and the mincing driveway, whose disclosures on the signing documents certainly came with warnings of whines, plosives, and yoga-like dragon breaths done at a fever pitch above. And now here those homeowners are, staring at my little yellow machine with dismay. It can only be akin to living full time in a crowded restaurant, leaning forward to hear what your family is saying, ceasing talk completely with the shriek of laughter at the next table. Below they are waiting for me to land, not knowing that, sorry, I will probably touch down lightly, exhale, then rev my engine and take off again.

25

Communication

This was the conversation in the cockpit of Air Florida Flight 90 right before departure from Washington National Airport one stormy winter day in 1982:

COPILOT: Look how the ice is just hanging on his, ah, back, back there, see that?
CAPTAIN: Side there.
COPILOT: See all those icicles on the back there and everything.
CAPTAIN: yeah.
...
COPILOT: Let's check these tops again since we been setting here awhile.
CAPTAIN: I think we go here in a minute.
COPILOT: That doesn't seem right, does it? (Three-second pause.) Ah, that's not right. (Two-second pause.) Well ...
PILOT: Yes, it is, there's eighty.

COPILOT: Naw, I don't think that's right. (Seven-second pause.) Maybe it is.
CAPTAIN: Hundred and twenty.
COPILOT: I don't know.

If you are not an aviator, this conversation probably makes little sense. Here's what's happening: The copilot is trying to get the captain to pay attention to ice accumulating on the wings. He points to the ice itself, then, as they begin their final run-up, he calls attention to the instruments. In deference to the captain's authority, the copilot never states outright that this is a bad situation. He drops continual hints, but the captain seems oblivious. As takeoff becomes imminent the icing problem remains unresolved, but the copilot stays locked into what linguists call a *conversational ritual*. Conversational rituals are hardwired into an interaction; they are a way of speaking (often unconsciously) agreed on by a subculture. People of similar ages have common conversational rituals, as do those of similar ethnicity, religion, gender, country, or even the same region. Certain group dynamics call for certain conversational rituals.

In the cockpit, the captain calls the shots while the copilot is there to assist; this dynamic has a clear conversational ritual. Recognizable, for instance, is the indirect language a subordinate intentionally uses to acknowledge the power differential. Recognizable too are the pauses calibrated to allow the superior—in this case the captain—to have his *Aha!* moment, and then to take (undue) credit for (finally) realizing the problem.

But the conversational ritual was not working. The captain continued to ignore the circumstances—specifically, that ice on wings leads to loss of lift—and yet the copilot could not bring himself to switch to a more urgent tone or to use direct statements. He could not break out of his conversational ritual. The plane pulled out onto the runway.

This interaction was transcribed by the flight data recorder, also known as the "black box." It was dug from the wreckage of Air Florida, which crashed on takeoff.

. . .

When I first read this chilling exchange, in the linguist Deborah Tannen's excellent book *Talking 9 to 5: Women and Men at Work*, it haunted me. How could two pilots—in this case both male—be brought down by rote courtesy? Surely the urgency of the icing situation allowed for a breach—a leap, really—out of conversational convention. But according to the aptly titled *The Quantitative Study of Communicational Success: Politeness and Accidents in Aviation Discourse* by the linguist Charlotte Linde, this playbook unfurls again and again—a subordinate foresees disaster, sticks to an entrenched conversation ritual, and the result is tragic.

Upon hearing this anecdote most people quickly conclude that direct communication would have averted the Air Florida crash. Surely the copilot should have abandoned his mealy-mouthed patter and yelled *De-ice the effing plane!* Why he didn't do this seems baffling. But Tannen tells us that conversational rituals are hard to break free from, partly because they are so unconscious, and partly because they are there for good reason. In this case it seems clear, however. This was a conversation ritual, abjectly failing.

Tannen cites Linde's work when she reminds that words have multiple uses; they have what may be called a "propositional" layer (the basic meaning), but they also have a "relational" side, which dictates the way those propositions are strung together. Tannen uses the example of traditional greetings: When someone says "How are you?" you are not expected to expound on the state of your bad knees or the irritating day you had at work. Instead, the ritual response (in America at least) is "Fine, how are you?" A greeting is not informational, but relational; it telegraphs *I see you, we are safe together.*

When Linde studied cockpit efficiency and safety, she may have approached it wondering whether the conversational ritual itself was a hazard. Instead, she found something surprising: crews who consistently used indirect communication rituals like that on the Air Florida flight performed best together. These conventions show respect while also maintaining order; haphazard interference by direct communication may lead to mistrust, confusion, and more accidents, not fewer, she concluded. And yet the interaction on the Air Florida flight had still gone so wrong.

The answer lay here: The conversational ritual remains an important relational tool. The key lies not in overturning it, but in *becoming better at it*—specifically, those in power needed to be more highly attuned to subordinates. After all, in the above transcription, the copilot never obscured that icing was present. Within the ritual he was being very clear. The real issue was the captain's unwillingness to properly listen.

. . .

Pilots who fly alone in the cockpit don't have to consider relational needs. When I reach out to other humans, say, air traffic controllers, I simply follow a version of the five W's: Who I speak to (*Santa Rosa tower*); Who I am (*experimental gyro [tail number here]*); Where I am (*ten miles south, at one thousand two hundred*); What I want (*inbound for landing*); Weather (*confirming that I understand the conditions, runways in use, and general protocols, having* listened to, say, *Information Kilo*). Each transmission must take up as little airtime as possible, and so subtext is pared away, complexity removed, adornment banished. It is worth noting that pilots also never say their name when in the air but rather that of their aircraft, and controllers present only as "tower" or "ground." This aids in clarity; we shed our humanness and with it that human tendency to obfuscate, elongate, or offer random poetics.

There is one exception to this transmogrification from human to inanimate in the cockpit. During a mayday call over the radio, the pilot will state—or air traffic control will inquire—how many people are on board, presumably so rescuers are prepared. But the term isn't "people." The term is "souls." Some find this disturbing, perhaps because it reminds that there is an ineffable part of us and it hovers uncertainly during a crisis, in a liminal space only tenuously attached to a body. It says *This is an emergency that might not end well.* But I find it profoundly moving, how the practical, almost cold, phraseology of pilotspeak veers suddenly into the spiritual.

The history of "souls" is murky, and the term does not currently appear anywhere in FAA handbooks, but air traffic controllers use it anyway, nomenclature handed down to them by their predecessors and enshrined in aviation culture. Some say it comes from the marine world, where the Morse code letters for aid, SOS, meant Save Our Souls as well as Save Our Ship. It was common for boats to be carrying dead bodies, so the distinction of "souls" was less a religious connotation and more for simple clarity. Today the term "souls" applies to all living humans on board an aircraft—passengers and crew—but it is worth noting that it does not include your faithful support animal.

One soul on board, I would say, if I were to issue a mayday call. *One soul, hoping for the best.*

Why Fly

For many pilots it is comforting to cede separation, takeoff, and landing procedures to air traffic controllers. I understand why: efficient orders are barked from all-seeing control towers and all we must do is respond and obey. But I don't fly into big airports much, so I often get quietly unnerved. Controllers tend to talk quickly, and if the airspace is busy, there is pressure not to misunderstand (one tip is to keep your own transmissions on the slower side and carefully enunciated; often the controller will mirror your style). Comprehension is so paramount in the traffic pattern that there is even a specific pronunciation for the numbers three and five and nine, so that nothing is misheard (*tree* and *fife* and *niner* respectively). In addition, the pilot must repeat back the given instructions each time. If you miss an important point on that playback, the controller reinstructs, and the result is an embarrassing seesaw as you try again to parse and echo the salient points in the stream of information coming at you. If you have the bad luck to get a tired or annoyed controller, their impatience with you and your shoddy hearing or rusty communication technique comes across in their tone; in other words, the relational creeps back in, thumbing its nose at the efforts of staid language to keep it out. Then you (I) become even more flustered, filling space with hesitant *ers* and *ums* audible to all the other pilots in the pattern. The air traffic controller harrumphs, you stammer, but neither can get away from the other until everything has been repeated correctly. When the controller finally releases you from her grasp, you (I) sigh with relief, sent onward and upward with the words "Good day," also heard as "G'day," and this tiny, positive, relational offering is something we also repeat back, sometimes with small variations, like *Hey buddy, thank you, g'day.*

Communication with the tower can't help but recall a couples counseling session, in which one party explains an issue and the other's only instruction (by a worn-out therapist sitting in front of both) is to listen, then repeat back what has been said. I have practiced this with my own wife, amazed how each time she visibly relaxes at the echo of her own words. It turns out that a lot of strife begins with the feeling of being unheard. Then it builds with ensuing miscommunication. How simple, then, just to listen closely. And now all should be well, you are in the traffic pattern separated from that Piper, that Lear, that experimental Velocity. *Cleared to land*, you are told. *Cleared to land*, you repeat perfectly. And yet it somehow doesn't work that way. There remains something terrifying about saying who I am, where I am, and what I want, when back on earth.

Here is a conversation from the imaginary black box of my relationship:

ME: Do you want to . . . go on a picnic this weekend, or next? (Real meaning: *Show me you want to make time for me.*)
SHE: I have to work. (Real meaning: *Not interested in making time.*)
ME: Okay, well . . . (Real meaning: *WTF, you have to work every single hour into the foreseeable future?*)
SHE: If it's important to you, I don't know, I can look at my schedule . . . (Real meaning: *I know it's important to you, but I want you to actually say it, though chances are the answer will still be no.*)
ME: No, don't bother. It's no big deal. (Real meaning: *I love picnics. But I feel sullen, and defensive, and I'm going to shut down right now.*)

Why Fly

SHE: I'm just so busy these days. (Real meaning: *I know you love picnics more than anything. But I don't really want to bother anymore.*)

ME: Okay. (Real meaning: *I see you don't want to bother anymore.*)

It doesn't take a linguist to discern the state of our communication. Our words meandered, were often garbled, were heavy with subtext. Where was the clarity of pilotspeak? Where was our understanding of the weather? Couldn't every *tree* and *niner* be perfectly clear across the static? But no. We were locked into this conversational ritual: of a marriage in decline. We could have taken Linde's advice. We could have *listened*. Listened as if our lives depended on it. But by the time we realized that—and we eventually did—neither of us wanted to. We had accumulated anger and disappointments like ice on wings and we simply barreled forward, two souls with eyes fixed on the promise of our own destruction.

26

Landing, You Can Do It Too

Colton Harris-Moore was seventeen years old when he rolled a Cessna 182 out of its hangar, got in, and taxied it to runway 34. The quiet Orcas Island runway faced Puget Sound; Harris-Moore would have seen its gray-green maw kick and foam under the Cessna's wheels just after takeoff. He turned crosswind, then headed south.

Nothing is remarkable about this. Except that Harris-Moore had never flown a real plane before. He had never actually been in a plane of any sort. But here he was in the air, maneuvering through busy Sea-Tac airspace. Behind him were a broken lock on a stranger's hangar, teams of sheriff's deputies searching for him after he had walked away from a minimum security detention center weeks before, his beloved dog Melanie, and presumably the many pilot instruction books he had scoured to prepare for this day, as well as the Microsoft video game that circa

Why Fly

this date in 2008 taught you to "fly" a Cessna 182—this exact plane—from the comfort of your living room.

Harris-Moore headed to the Cascade range, where that morning the conditions were about to be particularly loathsome. Veteran pilots who fly the area regularly told reporters later that it was "almost unbelievable" that he did not crash. Indeed, by the time Harris-Moore approached the mountains at an altitude of over 10,000 feet, winds were seething at sixty miles per hour over the ridgetops, "exploding against the little Cessna like aerial depth charges," according to the colorful description by the journalist Bob Friel. The turbulence "grabbed the little Cessna 182, shook it, twisted it, threw it down toward the jagged peaks of the Cascade mountains, then slammed it back up again," he imagines; Friel would later write a book about Harris-Moore and his string of crimes, which included stealing boats and cars and living undetected in the wilderness for stretches of time while plundering vacation cabins for food, showers, and eventually electronics, credit cards, and jewelry.

I was less interested in Harris-Moore's felonious behavior—which started when he was ten years old and stemmed from a childhood of neglect and abuse—than in his flying feats. Errors will be forgiven if you have an instructor in the right seat, or you have enough experience to react, as we know. Harris-Moore had neither. Yet he took off without stalling and maneuvered the purloined Cessna through terrible mountain turbulence (cops later found vomit all over the cockpit). More incredibly, he brought the plane back down to earth, landing some hours after takeoff. Well, not landing. Crash landing. He picked a field surrounded by beckoning wilderness and few people and then the plane came in fast, too fast, the wheels hitting hard. The plane bounced upward again, then down—this "ballooning" is a common beginner mistake—then finally tipped forward and augered, propeller shrieking, into a ditch. Harris-Moore was uninjured, but he had totaled the 182.

What amazes most about Harris-Moore was how he managed not just the technical skill of flying, but the psychological one. He stayed calm while being cannonballed into the air, not a sensation you can anticipate with a gaming platform. The cramped cockpit didn't fill him with dread, and he folded his six-foot-five frame into the pilot seat for hours. Mostly he floated for the first time above all that was familiar, yet didn't panic. I have spent many hours in different aircraft, yet it is not uncommon even now for me to shake my head to dispel a momentary disorientation, the uncanniness of being suspended in sky. In my paraglider, I remember periodically gazing at the lines that ran upward from my harness, as if to affirm that they would hold me there, under that thin, bright canopy. In my trike, I might tap the seat buckle that belted me in, just to be sure it was firmly closed. These were not so much safety checks as rituals, small gestures of humility, as a Catholic might air-draw a cross over her chest. It was part of a larger conversation I sometimes had with myself in the air, that wide-eyed disbelief at being airborne, not fear, really, but something that bordered on it—uncertainty, mortality, existential wonder.

Harris-Moore isn't the only one confident that he can fly a plane without formal lessons or experience. In a recent poll— one that specified the landing of a passenger plane—almost half the men said, *Sure, landing that, no problem.* One in five women polled also said yes. (Other surveys by this data analytics company showed men repeatedly and consistently more confident about successfully performing the Heimlich, say, or about defining what a tariff is.) There was a caveat in this poll: air traffic control would be there to talk the brave hero/heroine through it.

Why Fly

Still, it's confounding, and also a little bit wonderful, that *anyone* with zero flying experience thinks they could walk into the cockpit of a jetliner and keep from killing all souls on board. Does this cocksure civilian fully grasp what it is like to wrap fingers around the throttle, grip the yoke, dance the pedals, all the while deciphering the disembodied voice in the headset directing left, right, up, down, center, to that switch on the panel that must then be flipped, pulled, pressed, noted, turned? Then, as you, sir, descend to the stiff unyielding surface of our planet, you must believe in the sorcery that is the touchdown, that witchy alchemy of increasing gravity over lift that ends with wheels on asphalt. It's this part that is the most difficult. Try to sit in any cockpit during a landing, big jet or tiny gyrocopter. Watch the ground widen in the windshield like an incoming fist. Keep your stomach from bouncing, your throat from wheezing. At the right moment, you must level out, skimming the runway and yet still dropping—bleed off that airspeed, whippersnapper—with the air traffic controller's voice still keening, and the plane's avionics ringing and warning and chiming in your ear. Slow, slow, then at the precise moment, pull the nose up (but not too much up), and don't do this late or the ground delivers its knockout blow, but not too early or you will drop like a stone. The shriek of rubber on surface—who is dying after all of this? you may wonder—and then the shimmy as the brakes engage, the exhale of the breath you've been holding, the applause in your headset, the cries of grateful passengers, and your own hands flung over your head in victory, or so you want to do but you can't let go of the yoke, not yet, not yet. All in all, you, fair citizen, will finally know what students of flight have been wailing about for hundreds of years: coming home is so difficult, both technically and emotionally.

Landing, You Can Do It Too

In 1948, two perps stole a plane. They flew the two-seater Ercoupe 120 miles before touching down in Cheyenne, Oklahoma, in what the trooper who eventually arrested them said was "a perfect landing." This feat was astounding not only because the fugitives had never flown before, but because the pilot, Jimmy Bodard, was eleven years old. His accomplice, Ronny Peterson, was twelve. Jimmy told his captors with a shrug that he had learned to fly from reading comic books, and that it was "easy." After all, the youngster explained, not only were the comic books clear, but "there's a button with the word 'starter' over it and of course we knew about throttles and such things." He seemed baffled that the troopers hadn't read these comic books and attempted to fly a plane too.

This event kick-started what would become a national hysteria. But the hysteria was not, as you might think, against illegal plane flying. It was against comic books. Mid-twentieth-century comics did differ significantly from those of today, in which balloon-muscled superheroes fight for justice or friendly animals urge care and concern for trees and rivers. They were tawdry and violent, featuring true tales of gory crimes and hypersexualized illustrations of women. Congress lamented that comic books clearly incited "craven crime" in American youth. They set up an investigative subcommittee on the link between comic books and delinquency, though as far as I can tell they never looked deeply into testing how easy it was to read one and then actually take flight.

The boys were lucky in the airplane they picked to steal: the Ercoupe was simple to fly. Simpler than driving a car, or so the company claimed. It was also unusually stable, allegedly righting itself if it was inadvertently miscontrolled; the company's print

Why Fly

ads boasted that the plane was "certified incapable of spinning by the U.S. Civil Aeronautics Administration."

But what of the modern aircraft? How possible is it to land with little experience?

While I could not find an instance where a passenger plane had to be piloted by a civilian with no experience, people do make such landings in smaller aircraft. I recently listened to actual audio of an eighty-year-old talking to an air traffic controller after her pilot husband died in midflight. "This is a hell of a place to be," the new widow remarks dryly, her voice cracking only a little. "You're doing great, Helen," the controller answers, and tells her another plane is getting airborne to guide her in for a landing. "Someone better get here in a hurry," Helen answers, still calm, though of course she knows no one can really "get here." They can only fly beside her, try to instruct, hope she can follow despite the stress of a dead man (her husband!) in the next seat and the unfamiliar controls. Helen tells those helping her that day that she doesn't fly, but she did go through basic take-off and landing instruction, at her husband's urging. Yes, it was thirty years ago. And that plane had been nothing like this high-powered twin engine. Still, wasn't it better than nothing? Yes.

There is an aborted attempt. Then, re-entering the pattern, the plane runs out of gas. But still the octogenarian at the controls stays cool. This is about to be a no-second-chances landing. "Don't dive, Helen, don't dive," the assisting pilot cries as he watches her from his own plane behind, but of course Helen is going to push that nose down, inadvertently speed the aircraft up. How could she not? She is aiming for the ground, where all things are as they should be, not like up in the cockpit. But then Helen finds it in her to fight the get-on-the-ground-itis (good for you, Helen, some of us can't). She adjusts the nose, touches down. The plane lands safely, if fast, skidding off the runway and finally coming to rest in the grass.

Yvonne Kinane-Wells had not read comic books on flying. Nor did she have Helen's limited experience maneuvering a plane. She had only recently married her pilot husband, so I suspect that she had little passenger time in small aircraft too. But when her new husband had a incapacitating heart attack at 6,000 feet in October 2024, Kinane-Wells managed not to panic, and to follow the instructions given to her over the headset by air traffic controllers; she landed the plane without injury to herself or even to the aircraft (sadly, her husband did not survive).

Colton Harris-Moore himself never did master the landing. He stole four more planes in the ensuing two years and bonked them badly on his homecoming at least twice. Repeatedly, however, he walked away unharmed from each bouncing, skidding, nose-diving touchdown. In his defense, also, Harris-Moore was often attempting off-field landings, which differ greatly from those on runways, with their firm surfaces, windsocks, and lighted glide paths. Still, his final flight before capture (ending in another biffed landing) was again a daring one: from Bloomington, Indiana, to the Bahamas. This meant flying over not just ocean, but the Bermuda Triangle. As he circled the Sandy Point airport on Great Abaco, knowing that the local customs officers would ask unwelcome questions, he looked for an off-field opportunity. The open space he chose turned out to be a swamp. Upon touching down, the Cessna's wheels quickly mired, flipping the whole plane violently forward. Harris-Moore was unhurt again, but he had triggered the emergency landing transmitter, sending news of a crash to aviation authorities. His saga continued through a few more days, many stolen boats, several islands, some break-ins for soda and candy bars, and his

Why Fly

own inexplicable self-sabotage (he boasted to locals about who he was and dared them to call the police, claiming to be bored when he wasn't being hunted). Finally, stuck on a sandbar at night during a boat chase, Colton "the Barefoot Bandit" Harris-Moore surrendered to the police surrounding him. He had landed on earth for good—or at least until the end of his eventual seven-year prison sentence. He was released in 2016, and no records of further flying felonies seem to exist.

27

Final Approach

The day we end our relationship for good is ordinary. There are no big revelations, no sudden betrayals. We are already trying a thoroughly modern arrangement that, like aviation, has its own grating acronym—LAT (living apart together); we have separate domiciles now, but otherwise remain monogamous partners.

I sit on the couch in her place. She asks lightly, "How long are we going to keep doing this," and laughs. She expects me to say *forever* and laugh back. Instead, I say slowly, "No longer. We should stop." She pales at how unexpected this is. And how right it sounds.

We cry.

There is no declaration of an emergency. There is no wild panic. There is no spectacular crash. After fifteen years together, we begin to bring the plane toward a gentle touchdown on a runway we have been circling, circling, for too long now.

28

Touchdown

In 1980, a volcano in Washington State called Mount St. Helens erupted. It wasn't unforeseen; more than ten thousand seismic tremors were recorded in the preceding weeks, and steam had begun to vent. But like anything dramatic, the explosion was still shocking. Lava sheared 1,300 feet off the peak and scorched 230 surrounding square miles. A muscular plume of hot ash shot fifteen miles into the air. Fifty-seven people died. It left a mile-wide crater and a gray film of devastation that still lingers. I can't yet see this devastation from my perch, one thousand feet in the air, forty years later, but I am flying up a valley toward it.

This is my first ever "cross-country," meaning a multi-airport, multi-state, multi-day trip, and it is just months after my wife and I are officially over. The plan is that Paul will fly the first leg, bringing our shared aircraft from our hangar in California to Seattle; I will make the return trip to our home airport. Each leg will take three days, three states, some large mountain ranges, and a dozen or so airports. This adventure resonates, and intimidates. My marriage is over, and I am in a strange liminal place that needs a map, a compass, and a way to get a long view over unfamiliar terrain. Planning and executing a gyrocopter adventure seems relevant.

Otherwise, what handbook do I have on how best to shed a person, and a life?

When I was a firefighter, I had several tactics for dealing with grief, none of them particularly effective. After a difficult day, I might sit in my car alone and cry. A difficult day was this: CPR on a baby. A father who waited for (bad) news of the toddler still inside the fire building and who tugged on my sleeve as I exited to refill my air pack, wanting to hear of his son's safe rescue (no). The six bodies my crew had to uncover from the rubble of an apartment blaze—two adults, four children. The woman who was catatonic in a church pew, whom I recognized, because it was her baby I had performed that CPR on just the week before.

Or grief just seeped up, like a contaminated chemical bubbling and pooling at a Superfund site. *Holy cow, contaminated chemicals*, one might say, pointing. But it's a Superfund site after all, of course there are contaminated chemicals. An ad on television might trigger, perhaps a rollicking puppy who played on the now very clean floor near the very efficient cleaning materials in the very sparkling house: I'd tear up. Or how about the all-wheel-drive car looping along stunning cliffside road, ocean glinting behind, pure elegance and mettle, no money down, zero percent APR: weep just a little.

"No wonder no one can tell you how to do it," writes Alexandra Fuller in her book *Fi*, about mourning the sudden and unimaginable death of her teenage son. "Clearly no one, no friend, no family, no benign stranger, would come to lift this weight off of us, these bulldozers, these tomb boulders. It was up to us, up to me, to find my way out, to melt, thaw, and resolve."

The loss of a marriage is not the death of a child. Let's be clear. But I too needed to melt, thaw, and resolve.

When Paul arrives at the small airport near Seattle, he can only murmur a tired greeting, then stiffly proceed to unpack. Hundreds of miles in an open cockpit can kick the shit out of you, that was plain as day. I give him an enthusiastic high-five and hug anyway, and he leaves to catch a passenger plane home. My own journey starts the next day; I am wildly nervous, and it shows in the way I fuss over every item on the preflight checklist and intermittently wipe sweaty palms on my flight suit.

The planning of the trip had been easy enough. I would need to skirt large airports like Seattle and Portland and Sacramento International, as well as some military bases. I would pick terrain that offered bailout spots if necessary (not always possible) and then add any sights I might want to see (Paul would divert east to fly over Crater Lake but I decided to keep my trip simple). I would be in the air for no longer than about an hour and a half at a stretch, after which one starts to tire, whereupon I would land, shake off the wind and the noise, tend to bodily needs. I researched the small airports en route: Did they have fuel? Could I park overnight? I mapped out alternate routes; if there was no fog on the coast, I might head that way. If I decided not to land there, could I land here? I booked places to stay for the three nights away.

Mostly, though, I fretted. How burly would the wind be here? What was the chance of low ceilings there? Should I zig then zag, or zag then zig? It became stupid. Dozens of new airports, great swaths of territory I had never flown, high passes to cross. I went to sleep anxious. I woke up anxious. I was enough of a pilot to be baffled by this feeling, but enough of a writer to immediately understand it. I was living a metaphor, displacing my anxiety about my life onto that of the trip I was about to take. I needed to get a better handle on the new trajectory I faced, so of course I decided instead to concentrate on a gyro cross-country that would take only three days.

Anxiety, no matter its real source, is exhausting. I wanted to calm down, enjoy my gyro adventure, but how? Finally, I lit on a perspective that solved it for me.

Every airport I had ever flown into had been new to me once. I usually picked one within an hour or so of my own airport. I would peer at its tiny symbol on the map, read its relevant information, fly to it, land, take off, and fly back to home base. The excursion would take a few hours, and it felt exhilarating, a little nerve-racking, but totally doable.

This is no different, I told myself. It was just many new airports strung together all at once and a familiar protocol with each one: tune to the right radio frequency, fly overhead to check the wind direction, set up for the traffic pattern.

"What saves a man is to take a step," said Saint-Exupéry. "Then another step. It is always the same step, but you have to take it."

Step by same step, one airport at a time. That was the way to look at it.

I could do this.

I hadn't intended to divert toward Mount St. Helens; it is my first day and not on the flight plan. But Paul had been amazed by the tree stumps bristling the gray slopes, the logs sheared and lying flat as if they had been thrown there (they had). He had been wide-eyed about the crater. So when I see its hump in the distance to my left, I think *okay*.

My nerves, taut on departure, have loosened with each airport I've landed at, each refuel I've successfully negotiated. I have the daylight. I won't go too close. But I want to get a better look. The drainage I fly up has a milky vein of water. I keep it below me, liking the look of its broad sand bars in case of an emergency landing. Ahead, the peak outlines itself with snow. I keep shaking my head, a little overwhelmed. The looming mountain, its once incandescent rage; it was easy to imagine lava sliding down its flank like a furious reptile, the ash blurring the air, the belching innards of the planet heaving themselves upward.

But I turn south before I come to the blast zone. I am worried about fuel, and about deviating from the plan. I'm someone who likes a plan, and this is my first cross-country trip, and I don't want to do anything that could cascade into pilot error: *Oh yeah, she got a little confident, decided to do a side trip, and then, well, you know how that goes.*

In hindsight, I should have continued, caught at least the outer scrim of devastation, some of those petrified matchstick trees, a glimpse of that concussed landscape, any proof that when something blasts apart it leaves a wasteland, but that even this wasteland can exist as something, just different-shaped, say, lopsided and scooped out, but still unmistakably itself, a mountain.

But: *Fuel*, I remind myself. I tap my GPS screen and input a straight line to the next airport.

I land at a sleepy airfield already regretting that I hadn't continued. Two pilots peer from a hangar, then walk around Woodstock wobbling hands on chins and saying "Heard about these, never seen one." This has happened at almost every pit stop; the curiosity at such a strange craft, the questions that are really statements (*So it's turbocharged, looks like/Goes about 90 at

Why Fly

cruise, right?), the ritual of milling, the surprise that I've flown all the way from Seattle, heading all the way to California, the subsequent recalibration of who I am, some more nods. Then refuel, wave, take off. I do this again and again, step and step and step, and when I ultimately land that first night, I am soaringly happy, happy like a puppy, happy in a steep, endocrine-induced way, a windblown, tired, brave-explorer, grinning-wide way. I tie down Woodstock and feel (undeservedly) like Saint-Exupéry unrolling a blanket to sleep under his plane in the desert (I go instead to a hotel).

That evening, I walk along a pretty river and stop for a celebratory glass of wine. As I take my seat, I am already erasing the once future in which I would have texted a photo of the wine to my wife with some caption like *Celebrating!* and she would have texted back *Yay! How do you feel?*

I feel so proud, I would have texted back.

Heart emoji, she would respond. *I'm so proud of you. Come home safe please.*

Instead, I text Paul.

Landed happy at Corvallis! Had a nice day.

Understatement, simplicity. This was pilotspeak texting.

Congrats he writes back immediately. *That's a really cool thing to have done, no?*

I read the text, feeling a slow bloom of gratitude.

I think of my day, which was more than nice, more than happy. And then I text back.

I feel so proud.

On day two I once again cross mountain ranges veined with logging roads and scythed of trees in startling swaths, seemingly haphazardly. Rivers stumble along iridescent valleys. A touch and go at this airport just to say I'd done it, a landing at that airport to refuel. Hay rolled into cylindrical bales looking like breakfast buns. Towns clumped along roads. One barn, brake-light red, right out of a movie set. An orange tabby only half opening its eyes when I enter the pilot shack, unimpressed. Low ceilings that mean I scud at 500 feet, uncertain whether I can make it over the next pass, but then the clouds lift, and I do, and I did, and I land again for fuel.

A moment of appreciation now for the lowly touch and go, that arrival that is not quite an arrival, where you stroke the tires along the runway, maybe settle them completely, slow, then accelerate to take off again. The touch and go is the aviation equivalent of saying hello, hand up in a wave, but not stopping to chat; it is a rakish greeting, a fleeting connection. You almost want to put two fingers to the brim of your helmet in that devil-may-care salute as you lift skyward again (don't). The touch and go allows the pilot to practice landings without the inefficiencies of coming to a stop, pulling off the runway, taxiing back to the run-up area, and taking one's place in line again. But on this cross-country, it is also the way to notch a belt, each notch trumpeting *I landed there, and there, and there*, with the puffed-up pride of a conqueror but without doing much in the way of actual conquering.

On my last day I cross the border into California. These are roads I regularly drive when I visit my family. Finally, a landscape that is familiar. And yet from this height unfamiliar too, a new angle, everything seen askance. Dormant Mount Shasta lounges off to my left, always visible from the freeway, now surrounded by neatly arranged baby volcanoes that remind of road cones. The huge reservoir that fills me with dread when I drive over it—not from its hugeness but because it is a bellwether of just how little rain we've had that year, with its brown walls and boat

Why Fly

docks that hang in midair—is now a gentle brushstroke of blues and blacks (and miraculously filled to the brim after a winter of downpours).

The Cascades give way suddenly to the Central Valley. This is a wide plain that from my perch at 6,000 feet recalls a path made by some celestial snowplow, with drifts of mountains off to its distant sides—the Sierra Nevada to the east, the Coast Range to the west. Honestly, the Central Valley is a place I dislike when on the ground—too hot, too windy, too flat, too brown, too etched and stitched by farmland that repeats and repeats like a stutter. Too many towering fast food signs, too many malls, too many block houses with dry yards against dusty haze.

From this altitude, though, I meet the Central Valley on its own stalwart terms, that is to say, its geologic terms; it is suddenly clear how subduction and upwarping and silting formed this place, how it was once an inland sea. How could I not admire this proud plain of land, this stoic elder, spattered with the past? It is a landscape shaped by its afflictions: the soft shoe moves of unseen tectonic plates (although it contains no earthquake faults itself, there are many nearby), the molten hysterics of a planetary inner core, the slicing and sluicing of rain, the gobbling wind, the truncheon that is the sun. Add to that the many puny indignities inflicted on it by humans, that redirecting of rivers, that tilling of soil, that laying of roads, of fences, of dams. It looks beautiful to me now, this languid expanse that unfurls for 450 miles, indifferent, unperturbed. shrugging at the pummeling and shaking and battering. *Is that all you got?*

Further proof, this valley is, that forces don't have to sandblast you out of existence, just change, fortify, perhaps replenish. Not that the wounds don't scar, have consequences. Here a deep wandering crack that was once a river, there a tipped-over hillside, not to mention the increasing sag, which I can't see but I know about. The floor of the Central Valley is dropping by as much as a foot every year, the result of the ravenous suckling of its underground water by humans. But the valley seems unbothered. It was once an inland sea, why not now be a falling weft of desiccated rock and sand? *I have no particular need of water*, it might as well be saying, *you go ahead and drink yourself out of existence, I will still be here, a millennium on.*

I circle and land at the tiny Haigh airport, pronounced *hey*, so that every call I make in the traffic pattern sounds like a jaunty salutation: *Hey traffic, experimental gyro ten miles out at 1,000 inbound, hey, traffic, hey, hey.* It's now 90 degrees on the ground—a 40-degree difference from where I was just hours ago. In a single day I've experienced a whole life, through all these landscapes: I've whiplashed from 500 feet to 6,000 to scud clouds and leap passes. I've gone from smooth air to turbulence. I've crossed from greenery to copper, from mountain ranges to desert plains. I've shivered in Oregon, now I sweat in midday California.

I pull off outer layers, chat with an airport manager, take off again. I turn west and the desert flats finally meet a high upwelling of rock. On the other side the topography becomes scrub oak and hills and lakes. I am finally back to familiar flying territory. I think I can smell the ocean.

When I land at my home airport it is without fanfare, with no one to greet me. I am tired, disheveled, jangling from the heat and the wind and the engine noise. I untangle myself from my headset, get out of the cockpit gingerly. I stand in front of my hangar. I pat my pockets looking for my phone to send the requisite texts that assure I have landed safely. But it's also as if I am checking that I am still here, the me that left days ago.

It would be facile to say that I am somehow reborn. Yet how could I not be affected by hours upon hours skimming ablation, eruption, subduction, erosion, those mighty but indifferent assaults on our unperturbable earth. Three days of reading a geologic self-help book. Three days that emphasize what a scratch I am in this white space called cosmos/universe/forever.

Subsidence now, a big rain soon enough. Silt to fill gaps, erosion to regap them. Change, the landscape tells me, is inevitable; you, tiny thing, will survive it.

I send a text to my family, my ex-wife included, with a photo of me smiling stupidly in front of my hangar, telling them I landed safely.

I send a text to Paul, same photo, also telling him that I landed intact. Then I tack on a sentence left out of the family missive: *Let's plan another one.*

Hangar

Push the gyro to the hangar now. Wipe the rotors down, clean the windshield of bugs (say a prayer for the bugs), fill the gas tank, strip off the flight suit, write down the hours flown, scribble a quick description in handwriting so windblown and stick-jostled that you probably won't be able to read it later anyway, charge the headset, step outside and notice the sky's newest version of blue (after every flight you are a freshly minted aficionado of hue and tint, of shade and glow and sparkle). Step back in, gather your earthly things: your purse, your phone, your ability to speak full sentences, your car remote, your water bottle, your manners, your sense of balance, your wry sense of humor, your stiff upper lip, your left brain, your right brain, your heart with its regular sinus rhythm. You are back to being an earthbound human. But not totally back, not really, because part of you is still up there and you are already counting the hours until you will return and reclaim her.

ACKNOWLEDGMENTS

A book is a journey, a long arc across a lonely sky. If you are lucky there are people back on earth cheering you on. I am lucky.

Much gratitude first and foremost to my agent, Charlotte Sheedy, and to my editor, Nancy Miller. You believed.

Thank you too to all the people at Bloomsbury who worked so hard to land this book safely. A special shout-out to Amanda Dissinger, my tireless and unflappable publicist.

My readers are indispensable: Bonnie Tsui and Sophia Raday, once again you offered invaluable advice. I couldn't be a writer without your help and friendship.

Thank you also to my twin, Alexandra Paul, my first reader and very biased supporter.

Thank you to my brother, Jonathan Paul, who understands my flying ventures, and to my mom, Sarah Paul, who doesn't understand them but supports them, though doesn't want to hear about them until they are over safely, because it taxes her nerves too much.

Thank you to Paul Hollingworth, who introduced me to gyrocopters, shares Woodstock with me, and generously read this whole book, offering valuable feedback. Don't know what I would do without you these days, my friend.

Thank you to my gyro flight instructors, Britta Penca and Dayton Dabbs. I hope I do you proud.

Thank you to editor Mark Lotto, who offers incisive advice.

Thank you to my friend Jon Mooallem, author of *Wild Ones*, one section of which I cover extensively in Chapter 9, and whose writing has always inspired and gobsmacked.

Thank you, Pierre Valette, for flagging Georgia O'Keeffe's obsession with clouds, and for being cool in general.

Thank you to the Writers Grotto, a community without which I would be a pipefitter or an office temp or a crossing guard or a frazzled insurance salesperson, anything but the writer I am today.

Thank you to the Mary Oliver estate, who granted these permissions:

"Starlings in Winter" by Mary Oliver. Reprinted by the permission of The Charlotte Sheedy Literary Agency as agent for the author. Copyright © 2003 by Mary Oliver with permission of Bill Reichblum.

"This Morning Again It Was in the Dusty Pines" by Mary Oliver. Reprinted by the permission of The Charlotte Sheedy Literary Agency as agent for the author. Copyright © 1992 by Mary Oliver with permission of Bill Reichblum.

Finally, to Wendy MacNaughton, who read the final manuscript with love and generously agreed to my version of our relationship on the page: as always, thanks for you.

NOTES

CHAPTER 1: SKY

003 **when my engine cuts out:** This incident is reworked from a similar essay I wrote for *Outside* magazine, July 2018, when various adventurers were asked to describe a notable first in their outdoor life. The article was titled "Caroline Paul on Her First Emergency Landing."

007 **"from the height of our rectilinear trajectories:** Antoine de Saint-Exupéry, *Wind, Sand, and Stars* (Reynal and Hitchcock, 1939).

CHAPTER 2: GRAVITY

013 **Don't be fooled by its clumsy name—gyrocopter/gyroplane:** "Gyrocopter" was trademarked by the Bensen Aircraft Corporation back in the 1950s. The technically correct term is *gyroplane*, but since both are widely used colloquially to denote the same machine, I use the term *gyrocopter* in the book, which I find more descriptive.

CHAPTER 3: CHECKLISTS

017 **Atul Gawande shares my enthusiasm:** Atul Gawande, "The Checklist," *New Yorker*, December 2, 2007, newyorker.com/magazine/2007/12/10/the-checklist.

018 **a cat emerged:** "Remove Cat Before Flight," youtube.com/watch?v=J_8mdH20qTQ.

Why Fly

019 **the list grew over the years:** Patrick Kiger, AARP blogs, May 22, 2013, blog.aarp.org/legacy/john-goddards-ultimate-bucket-list-life-achievement-ambitious-goals.

020 **the 51 percent rule:** Federal Aviation Regulations: Title 14, Code of Federal Regulations (14 CFR), part 21, section 21.191(g).

CHAPTER 4: HOW FLIGHT WORKS (BECAUSE IT DOES)

029 **but also acted upon by bigger forces:** For more on how weather works on a macro level, this podcast is enlightening: James Fodor, host, *The Science of Everything*, podcast, episode 109 "Weather Part I," August 1, 2020, and episode 110, "Weather Part II," August 30, 2020.

029 **to elevate their body temperature:** August Krogh and Erik Zeuthen, "The Mechanism of Flight Preparation in Some Insects," *Journal of Experimental Biology* 18, no. 1 (1941): 1–10, jeb.biologists.org/content/jexbio/18/1/1.full.pdf.

030 **Canada geese may engage in head tossing:** Dennis G. Raveling, "Preflight and Flight Behavior of Canada Geese," *The Auk*, 86: 671–81, October 1, 1969, Searchable Ornithological Research Archive, University of New Mexico, sora.unm.edu/sites/default/files/journals/auk/v086n04/p0671-p0681.pdf.

030 **a few warm-up launches:** B. Voelkl and J. Fritz, "Relation Between Travel Strategy and Social Organization of Migrating Birds with Special Consideration of Formation Flight in the Northern Bald Ibis," January 14, 2017, *Philosophical Transactions of the Royal Society* B 372: 20160235, royalsocietypublishing.org/doi/pdf/10.1098/rstb.2016.0235.

030 **scientists disagree over the physics:** Kenneth Chang, "Staying Aloft: What Does Keep Them Up There?" *New York Times*, December 9, 2003.

030 **no clear answer:** Ed Regis, "No One Can Explain Why Planes Stay in the Air," *Scientific American*, February 1, 2020.

032 **The physics professor Rhett Allain:** Rhett Allain, "There's No One Way to Explain How Flying Works," *Wired* magazine, February 22, 2018, wired.com/story/theres-no-one-way-to-explain-how-flying-works/.

032 **the agility of "a pregnant duck":** Michael Brooks, *The Art of More: How Mathematics Created Civilization* (Pantheon, 2022), 148.

033 **" 'Do nothing' is my first bit of counsel":** Mark Vanhoenacker, *How to Land a Plane* (New York: The Experiment, 2019).

CHAPTER 6: A SHORT, INCOMPLETE HISTORY OF FLIGHT

039 **The desire to fly:** Robert Bluffield, *Over Empires and Oceans: Pioneers, Aviators and Adventurers Forging the International Air Routes 1918–1939* (Great Britain: Tattered Flag Press, 2014), 1.

043 **traveled 900 meters:** Judy Rumerman, U.S. Centennial of Flight Commission, centennialofflight.net/essay/Prehistory/Cayley/PH2.htm.

CHAPTER 7: AIRBORNE

047 **When fixed wing pilot Marion Springer first saw a gyrocopter:** Marion Springer, *Born Free: My Life in Gyrocopters* (Springer Enterprises, 2004).

052 **Diane Ackerman says of flying:** Diane Ackerman, *On Extended Wings* (Atheneum, 1985), 8.

CHAPTER 8: LIFT

059 **Vanhoenacker lauds landings:** Mark Vanhoenacker, *How to Land a Plane* (New York: The Experiment, 2019).

Why Fly

CHAPTER 9: GLIDERS

064 **these four-ton behemoths:** *Pilot Training Manual for the CG-4A Glider*, AF Manual 50-17 (restricted), Headquarters Army Air Forces, Office of Flying Safety, digitalcollections.museumofflight.org/items/show/57893.

065 **part of almost every military campaign:** Major Leon Spencer, "Eight Missions," National WWII Glider Pilots Association, ww2gp.org/war/missions/.

066 **they decided to bring back a few of its vultures:** Hanna Reitsch, *The Sky My Kingdom* (Bodley Head, 1955), 72.

CHAPTER 10: MIGRATION

070 **joined by a flock of ducks:** Bill Lishman, *C'mon Geese*, video, 1990, williamlishmanartist.com/video/.

072 **Jon Mooallem captures:** Jon Mooallem, *Wild Ones: A Sometimes Dismaying, Weirdly Reassuring Story About Looking at People Looking at Animals in America* (Penguin Press, 2013).

074 **decided on the motored paraglider:** Nick Paumgarten, "Helicopter Parents," *New Yorker*, February 17 & 24 issue, 64.

CHAPTER 11: THE PIONEERS

077 **Turns out there were other female adventurers:** I only figured this out while researching my book for middle graders entitled *The Gutsy Girl: Escapades for Your Life of Epic Adventure* (New York: Bloomsbury, 2016). In it I highlight women adventurers around the world and back in time, the overall number of which surprised and delighted me.

078 **the inimitable Bessie Coleman:** Philip S. Hart, *Up in the Air: The Story of Bessie Coleman* (Trailblazer biography series, Lerner Publishing, 1996).

078 **she was wildly famous:** Amelia Earhart, *The Fun of It* (reprint, Academy Chicago Publishers, 2006).

CHAPTER 12: LONELINESS

085 **Baumgartner's eventual leap:** John Tierney, "24 Miles, 4 Minutes and 834 M.P.H., All in One Jump," *New York Times*, October 14, 2012.

086 **aviation has always made progress:** Robert Curley, ed., *The Complete History of Aviation: From Ballooning to Supersonic Flight* (Britannica Educational Publishing, 2012).

086 **glued to Baumgartner's live feed:** "Felix Baumgartner Space Jump World Record 2012 Full Video," Red Bull Productions, 2012, https://www.youtube.com/watch?v=Oy-2LnAAhjA.

088 **Alan Eustace jumped quietly and without fanfare:** John Markoff, "15 Minutes of Free Fall Required Years of Taming Scientific Challenges," *New York Times*, October 27, 2014.

088 **tipped himself homeward:** Sadly, and a little ironically, given the extremity of most of his feats, Felix Baumgartner died July 17, 2025, in an accident during a routine paraglider flight.

CHAPTER 13: FEAR OF FLYING

089 **forty-five thousand domestic departures a day:** Federal Aviation Administration, "Air Traffic by the Numbers," United States Department of Transportation, faa.gov/air_traffic/by_the_numbers.

090 **one fatal crash:** International Air Transport Association Annual Safety Report, "2023: A Record-Breaking Year for Safety," February 28, 2024, iata.org/en/pressroom/2024-releases/2024-02-28-01/.

091 **For others it's the tight space, the closing doors:** Lisa McArty, "Afraid of Flying? Here's How to Make It Feel Less Scary," *New York Times*, October 16, 2024.

Why Fly

091 **Captain Steve Allright:** Sarah Lyall, "'The Plane Is Fine': An Airline Course Looks to Overcome Fear in the Skies," *New York Times*, April 2, 2024.
092 **Amanda Ripley wrote about disaster behavior:** Amanda Ripley, *The Unthinkable: Who Survives When Disaster Strikes, and Why* (Crown Archetype, 2008).

CHAPTER 14: THE VIEW

098 **This exposure is called the *overview effect*:** Yasmine Tayag, "Six NASA Astronauts Describe the Moment in Space When 'Everything Changed,'" *Inverse* magazine, March 27, 2018.
099 **in the documentary film *Overview*:** Guy Reid, director, *Overview* (Planetary Collective, 2012), youtube.com/watch?v=sKK4dAu_sFo.
099 **"We stand there gaping":** Samantha Harvey, *Orbital* (Grove Atlantic, 2023), 32, youtube.com/watch?v=sKK4dAu_sFo.
101 **with whole books that explain what triggers it:** I have written at length about awe in my book *Tough Broad: From Bird-Watching to BASE Jumping—How Outdoor Adventure Improves Our Lives as We Age* (New York: Bloomsbury, 2023).

CHAPTER 15: LOW AND SLOW

103 **O'Keeffe's first flight-inspired painting:** Grace Almanza, "Georgia O'Keeffe's Clouds and Skies," Mornings with O'Keeffe Lecture Series, Georgia O'Keeffe Museum, October 11, 2024.
104 **Langewiesche is also a fan of the bird's-eye view:** William Langewiesche, *Inside the Sky: A Meditation on Flight* (Vintage Books, 1998), 12.
107 **I was being cloud-sucked:** I have written about this hair-raising misadventure in my book *The Gutsy Girl: Escapades for Your Life of Epic Adventure* (New York: Bloomsbury, 2016).

110 **a champion paraglider named Dave Turner:** I wrote about this adventure for *Sunset* in 2015. Caroline Paul, "Above the Owens Valley," *Sunset* magazine, September 2015, page 62-63.

CHAPTER 16: BIRDS

115 **as the naturalist Helen Macdonald describes them:** Helen Macdonald, *Vesper Flights* (New York: Grove, 2020).

116 **"strayed toward me, transparent and whirling":** Annie Dillard, *Pilgrim at Tinker Creek* (Harper's Magazine Press, 1974), 41.

116 **follows seven or so nearby companions:** A. E. Goodenough, N. Little, W. S. Carpenter, and A. G. Hart, "Birds of a Feather Flock Together: Insights into Starling Murmuration Behaviour Revealed Using Citizen Science," *PLoS One* 12, no. 6 (June 19, 2017): e0179277, pmc.ncbi.nlm.nih.gov/articles/PMC5476259/.

117 **the behavioral scientist Iain Couzin:** John Seabrook, "Crush Point," *New Yorker*, January 30, 2011.

119 **what is called** *wave slope soaring*: I. A. Stokes and A. J. Lucas, "Wave-slope Soaring of the Brown Pelican," *Mov Ecol* 9, no. 13 (2021), doi.org/10.1186/s40462-021-00247-9.

120 **fifty thousand miles in a year:** Cornell Lab of Ornithology, Arctic Tern overview, allaboutbirds.org/guide/Arctic_Tern/overview.

120 **the bar-tailed godwit:** Robert E. Gill, "Extreme Endurance Flights by Landbirds Crossing the Pacific Ocean: Ecological Corridor Rather Than Barrier?" Royal Publishing Society, October 29, 2008, doi.org/10.1098/rspb.2008.1142.

122 **less well known is the innovative wing shape:** Alexandra Dean, director, *Bombshell: The Hedy Lamarr Story* (Kino Lorber Theatrical: Zeitgeist Films), shown on PBS American Masters series, May 2018.

CHAPTER 17: MAPS

124 **to get a sense of the architecture above:** To understand aviation airspace, I recommend the YouTube series by the pilot Donovan Batiste, youtube.com/@pilotdonovanbatiste. I also recommend Rod Machado's *Private Pilot Handbook*.

131 **John F. Kennedy Jr. got himself into:** Bruce Landsberg, "Landmark Accidents: Vineyard Spiral," AOPA newsletter, September 5, 2000.

132 **solely on the airplane's banked turn:** William Langewiesche, "The Turn," *Atlantic Monthly* 273, no. 6 (December 1993), 115–22.

CHAPTER 18: THE CONTROLS

135 **an all-female combat unit:** Bryan Holland, "Meet the Night Witches, the Daring Female Pilots Who Bombed Nazis by Night," *History.com*, July 7, 2017.

137 **Sometimes a bomb would "stick and not drop":** Ann Noggle, *A Dance with Death: Soviet Airwomen in World War II* (Texas A&M University Press, 1994).

CHAPTER 19: NAVIGATION

142 **described by Mark Vanhoenacker:** Mark Vanhoenacker, *Skyfaring: A Journey with a Pilot* (Knopf, 2015).

146 **Into this fray comes the U.S. Postal Service:** William Leary, *Aerial Pioneers: The US Mail Service, 1918–1927* (Smithsonian Institution, 1985).

147 **an air race from San Francisco to New York:** John Lancaster, *The Great Air Race: Glory, Tragedy, and the Dawn of American Aviation* (New York: W. W. Norton, 2023).

Notes

CHAPTER 20: WEATHER

162 **It was the "Hump" pilots of World War II:** Caroline Alexander, *Skies of Thunder: The Deadly World War II Mission over the Roof of the World* (New York: Viking, 2024).

CHAPTER 21: GROUNDSPEED

167 **The air races were key:** Keith O'Brien, *Fly Girls: How Five Daring Women Defied All Odds and Made Aviation History* (Mariner Books, 2018).

171 **These were civilian women with private pilot certifications:** Molly Merryman, *Clipped Wings: The Rise and Fall of the Women Airforce Service Pilots (WASPs) in World War II* (New York University Press, 2020).

172 **When it came to errors:** Jacqueline Cochran, "Report on Women Pilot Program," published as "Jacqueline Cochran Final Report," wingsacrossamerica.us/wasp/final_report.htm#overall%20accident%20rates.

CHAPTER 22: AIRSPEED

174 **Brendan Koerner in his book:** Brendan Koerner, *The Skies Belong to Us* (Crown, 2014).

176 **Rust left his home in West Germany:** Reuters, "Pilot Said to Have a Passion for Flying," *New York Times*, May 30, 1987.

177 **"if me, in a small aircraft, can go straight there":** Tom LeCompte, "The Notorious Flight of Mathias Rust," *Smithsonian* magazine, July 2005.

179 **Did Hitler secretly send him?:** According to Hugh Trevor-Roper, who wrote his investigation *The Last Days of Hitler* in 1945 using firsthand sources, the answer categorically is that Hitler had no part in arranging Hess's flight and was outraged when it happened.

Why Fly

179 **Reich leaders consistently overindulged in drugs:** Norman Ohler, *Blitzed: Drugs in Nazi Germany* (Houghton Mifflin Harcourt, 2017).

CHAPTER 23: TRAFFIC PATTERN

191 **"A landing," muses the author Mark Vanhoenacker:** Mark Vanhoenacker, *How to Land a Plane* (New York: The Experiment, 2019).

CHAPTER 25: COMMUNICATION

203 **when I first read this chilling exchange:** Deborah Tannen, *Talking from 9 to 5: Women and Men at Work; Language, Sex and Power* (William Morrow, 1994). The original transcription can also be found in the linguist Charlotte Linde's paper "The Quantitative Study of Communication Success: Politeness and Accidents in Aviation Discourse," *Language in Society* 17, no. 3 (September 1988), 375–99.

205 **the history of "souls" is murky:** "The Mystery of 'Souls on Board,'" National Air Traffic Controllers Association, November 4, 2016, originally published by the FAA, natca.org/2016/11/04/nov-4-2016-the-mystery-of-souls-on-board/.

CHAPTER 26: LANDING, YOU CAN DO IT TOO.

210 **"almost unbelievable" that he did not crash:** Bob Friel, "The Ballad of Colton Harris-Moore," *Outside Online*, December 29, 2009, outsideonline.com/outdoor-adventure/exploration-survival/ballad-colton-harris-moore/.

210 **Friel would later write a book:** Bob Friel, *The Barefoot Bandit: The True Tale of Colton Harris-Moore, New American Outlaw* (Hyperion, 2012).

Notes

211 **almost half the men said,** *Sure, landing that, no problem*: YouGov poll, "How confident are you that you could safely land a passenger airplane in an emergency situation, relying only on the assistance of air traffic control?" January 20, 2023, today.yougov.com/topics/politics/survey-results/daily/2023/01/02/fd798/3.

211 **this data analytics company:** Chris Stokel-Walker, "How YouGov Became the UK's Best but Most Controversial Pollster," *Wired*, November 28, 2019, wired.com/story/yougov-general-election-poll-mrp/.

213 **two perps stole a plane:** "Boys, 11 and 12, Fly Stolen Plane 120 Miles on Knowledge Obtained from Comic Books," *New York Times*, May 22, 1948, 17.

213 **against comic books:** Phoebe Judge, host, *Criminal*, podcast, episode 294, "For the Sake of American Youth," Vox media Podcast Network, November 22, 2024, thisiscriminal.com/episode-294-for-the-sake-of-american-youth-11-22-2024/.

214 **"Someone better get here in a hurry":** Pilot Debrief webcast, "80-Yr-Old Passenger Lands ENGINE OUT After Pilot Dies!" YouTube, youtube.com/watch?v=7QifqB_vIMM.

215 **Yvonne Kinane-Wells had not read comic books on flying:** Alia Shoiab, "Wife Lands Plane After Pilot Husband Suffers Mid-Flight Heart Attack," *Newsweek*, October 8, 2024, newsweek.com/wife-lands-plane-husband-heart-attack-1965516.

CHAPTER 28: TOUCHDOWN

220 **writes Alexandra Fuller in her book:** Alexandra Fuller, *Fi: A Memoir of My Son* (New York: Grove, 2024).

A NOTE ON THE AUTHOR

CAROLINE PAUL is the *New York Times* bestselling author of eight books, including *The Gutsy Girl: Escapades for Your Life of Epic Adventure*; *Tough Broad: From Bird-Watching to BASE Jumping—How Outdoor Adventure Improves Our Lives as We Age*; *Lost Cat: A True Story of Love, Desperation, and GPS Technology*; the memoir *Fighting Fire*, about becoming one of the first female firefighters in San Francisco; and the novel *East Wind, Rain*. She lives in San Francisco.